THE LITTLE, BROWN
GUIDE TO SILVER

SERGIO CORADESCHI

THE LITTLE, BROWN GUIDE TO SILVER

Little, Brown and Company
Boston • New York • Toronto • London

A LITTLE, BROWN BROOK
First published in Great Britain in 1994
by Little, Brown and Company

Copyright © 1994 Arnoldo Mondadori Editore S.p.A., Milan
English translation copyright © Arnoldo Mondadori Editore S.p.A.,
Milan
Translation by Jay Hyams
Typesetting by Christopher Hyams-Hart

A CIP catalogue record for this book is available from the
British Library

ISBN 0-316-90716-2

10 9 8 7 6 5 4 3 2 1

Printed and bound in Spain by Artes Gráficas Toledo, S.A.
D.L.TO:50-1994

Little, Brown and Company (UK) Ltd
Brettenham House
Lancaster Place
London WC2E 7EN

CONTENTS

INTRODUCTION

Silver enjoys an everlasting appeal in the applied arts. A noble metal that is beautiful and precious but above all ductile, it permits the creation of objects in a wide range of tastes, styles and artistic techniques.

This Guide to Silver places its subject within the context of its cultural background, socio-economic realities and the customs and fashions that determine the forms taken by artistic expression. The relationship between form and decoration is examined, with particular emphasis on both the decorative motifs of certain stylistic periods and on the evolution of various shapes. A deeper understanding is offered by the many line drawings accompanying the text.

Because the range of silver objects is so very broad, only domestic or "civilian" silver will be dealt with here, thus excluding—albeit with great reluctance—religious works. The illustrations depict items the reader is most likely to encounter on the antiques market, either in shops or at auction. In the case of celebrated pieces, most of which date to early periods, recourse has been made to museum holdings; but the works displayed in museums, while invaluable and illuminating, are also inaccessible, unique and therefore less indicative of the trends that were most widespread and that marked the majority of the silver objects made in each period.

Alongside the text are special boxed entries that provide information on the principal production techniques or on types of silver that are less familiar or worthy of special note; brief biographies of the most famous silversmiths are also included.

Beginning with the 17th century, each chapter ends with an analysis of the period's flatware—knives, forks, spoons. Hallmarks present a seemingly endless subject, and tables designed to guide the reader are provided. Much of this vast field is as yet unexplored, however, and those seeking further information should consult the numerous manuals dedicated exclusively to the identification, study and cataloguing of these marks.

This book is dedicated to inexperienced newcomers to silver and seasoned enthusiasts alike and aims to help the reader to identify styles, recognize and understand decorative motifs and analyze forms.

ANTIQUITY AND THE MIDDLE AGES

Cup with loop handle nailed to one side, decorated with nielloed gold leaves and 21 male heads aligned in profile. From a Mycenaean tomb, second half 16th century B.C.

The oldest works in silver

Because it can be worked so easily (pieces can be hammered together), silver began to appear early on in those countries to which it is native, often associated with copper. Copper was the first metal worked by man on the way to civilization, and silver came immediately after. Finds from the Neolithic age at Troy and from the areas of the Minoan and Mycenaean civilizations bear witness to the use of objects made of silver. Primarily ritual or celebratory vessels, these pieces are worked with the techniques of embossing and niello inlay. Unfortunately, silver perishes easily through contact with the chemicals present in soil, and almost all such early pieces have been lost. Minoan and Mycenaean art show a strong preference for vigorous forms with strong outlines, and made use of such a broad range of motifs that their influence endured for many centuries. The decoration is based on dynamically curved lines that give a sense of movement: circles, spirals, coils. The antennae of butterflies are rendered with coils, and the tentacles of octopuses form spirals; petals and leaves are arranged diagonally around discs presented in relief to create wheeling compositions. In addition to geometric and plant forms, a broad range of figures were used—human, animal and forms based on fantasy—and these have an immediate sense of natural reality. This art had no compositional framework within which the movements and shapes of figures could be rationally worked out, and instead approached every image with a direct and extraordinary naturalness that may seem irrational but was always full of feeling and originality. Intensive mercantile contacts and population movements spread the Mycenaean civilization first throughout the area of the Aegean and then into the eastern and central Mediterranean. New centers of silver production were concentrated on Cyprus, an island rich in the copper that served as the alloy for silver, in Syria, in Egypt and in Asia Minor. This expansion brought about a fusion of Mycenaean art with that of Asia, Egypt and, most of all, Phoenicia. In the region of Greece, at Athens and in Attica, a decorative style was developed involving broken lines that was expressed in geometric forms. This preference for the geometric can also be found throughout the area of northern Europe, along the Danube and Rhine and even in far-away Scandinavia.

Trade and the development of silverworking

The Phoenicians played a leading role in spreading

Eastern and Egyptian precious goods and decorative motifs. Their broad network of trade connections, considerable piratical operations and far-flung colonies spread their figurative culture along the coast of northern Africa up to Morocco and then into Spain, creating many commercial outposts and colonies, including Carthage. As these colonies grew and prospered they assumed increasing autonomy from their homeland, which came under Persian control in the 6th century B.C. and began to decline. The importance and economic power of Carthage came to dominate the entire western Mediterranean. Phoenician-Carthaginian designs spread to Malta, western Sicily, Ibiza and Sardinia, while Greek colonists from the peninsula of Chalcidice established themselves in eastern Sicily, on the coast of Ionia and in southern Italy.

This series of overlapping and interweaving contacts formed an intricate network of reciprocal influences that laid the basis for the region's new economic power: Etruria.

Niello

Niello is a technique of artistic decoration similar to inlaying. The procedure begins with a design engraved into a silver surface using a burin (pointed steel tool). These incised lines are then filled with a blackish mixture of silver, red copper, lead and sulfur (the name niello *is an Italian word based on the Latin* nigellus, *"blackish," a diminutive of* niger, *"black"). This is then heated and, after cooling, the surface of the silver is carefully scraped, leaving a coloured design in the lines filled with niello that stands out against the shiny silver background in a pleasing contrast. By altering the composition of the mixture, grey-blue, brown, or black designs can be obtained. The technique was used by the early Greeks and Romans,*

reached great heights in Byzantine Constantinople, and was then adopted by the Arabs because it lent itself well to the creation of their figurative decorations (the so-called arabesques). It was later used in the Rhine and Meuse areas (famous for reliquaries) and during the 15th century was an almost exclusive speciality of Italy, especially for religious silver. An outstanding example of this is the famous pax (now preserved in the Bologna picture gallery) in nielloed silver made by the painter and goldsmith Francesco Raibolini, known as Francia (c. 1450-1517). Later nielloed silver was used in the decoration of the plates that decorated the locks of firearms used by 16th- and 17th-century armies.

Etruscan silver

With its solid civil and political organization, Etruria established a series of commercial and cultural contacts with the distant Greek east, Anatolian and Phoenician, by way of a long chain of islands, trade centers and ports of call that formed both a great trade route and a bridge between the East and West. The eastern-style Phoenician objects that were imported through trade greatly appealed to the Etruscans. This is explained by the lively, exuberant nature of Etruscan taste, which took pleasure in imbuing objects in precious metal with the signs of luxury. The pieces in silver made during the so-called Orientalizing phase of Etruscan art show the strong influence of contact with Eastern cultures by way of the Phoenicians; but this gave way to the influence of the precision and formal elegance of Greek art, contacted through the production areas of Greek artisans in Magna Graecia. The most widespread objects were various kinds of vases: wide craters, urns with multiple handles, goblets, deep cups and phiales, slightly concave pateras of great artistic interest because they were decorated all over using the most refined techniques. These decorations range across the entire arc of figurative subjects, with powerful visual impact.

Greek silver

Silver saw only limited use in the Greek world of the classical period (from the 6th to 5th century B.C.) because the silver mines of Mount Laurium, near Athens, were exhausted and because the use of silver for coins reduced its availability for other objects. Silver was used primarily for the treasuries of famous temples, such as those of Apollo and Artemis, where vases, trays, amphoras, pateras and perfume-burners were amassed. Sadly, almost nothing has survived of this silver. An idea of Greek silver can be gleaned, however, by examining examples found in ancient Scythia (southern Russia along the coasts of the Black Sea), where embossed silver cups showing clear Hellenic influence have been found. Works in silver decorated with high-relief embossing based on distant Greek models can also be found among the Thracians in the southeastern tip of the Balkan peninsula, with spreading offshoots in Gaul and into northern Europe, but the Greek influence there has been so transformed it can no longer be traced back to formal or decorative models. The contact with the luxurious courts of the Orient that began with the

period of Alexander the Great brought new life to Greek-Hellenic silver, visible most of all in pieces made for the banquet table.

Roman silver

Silver came into more frequent use during the Roman period, particularly for ban-

quet furnishings. Famous collections of objects from the Augustan age include the so-called treasures of Hildesheim, Boscoreale, Berthouville and Pompeii. These intensely decorated pieces bear witness to the sculptural form taken by Roman metalwork during the imperial age. These rigorously realistic decorative motifs were taken from architectural ornamentation (volutes, vines, palmettes) and the statuary of human figures (heads, portraits and shapes from the animal world). Cups with curved handles, cylindrical beakers with slightly flared lips, mirrors, pitchers and plates are among the most common types.

Most of these pieces were made for show, to be displayed or given as gifts to prominent people or temples of famous cults. Their rich decoration and imposing forms were not meant for

ANTIQUITY AND THE MIDDLE AGES

daily table use, and although everyday silver objects existed, no trace of them remains. An important form of Roman silver was the large fully decorated plates that were made as table decorations and were customarily sent as gifts to high functionaries of the empire, to rulers of satellite states or even to the emperors themselves. In use until the 7th century A.D., these plates are believed to have been made in the artisan workshops of Constantinople, the richest imperial city.

Medieval silver

A guide to secular silver can say little about the Middle Ages, since almost no pieces of secular ware survive from that period. Pieces related to the functions of the church, however, are abundant: chalices, processional crosses, reliquaries, alms plates, thuribles, monstrances, even entire altars. As for secular ware, we can only refer to general stylistic characteristics and the more or less summary descriptions that can be gleaned from antique inventories. We know for certain that a great quantity of domestic silver existed, including water pitchers matched to basins, ornamental plates in the late-Roman tradition, amphoras and vases. All such pieces, however, were intended more for the ostentation of the banquet than for any functional use. In terms of stylistic decoration, the period went from the repetition of ancient classical models to the influence of Byzantine ornamentation to the stylistic elements of the incipient Gothic. The major centers of silver production were located in the area of the Meuse River and in Germany, with prolific schools at Cologne and Aachen. Gothic models moved from these centers to Portugal and Flanders, where they were further developed.

15TH- AND 16TH-CENTURY SILVER

The 15th century
The 16th century

Cup in gilt silver decorated with enamelled coats of arms, by Wenzel Jamnitzer, Nuremberg (c. 1540). The shape is reminiscent of wooden models from the Gothic period in Germany.

Opposite below left: Silver beaker, Amsterdam, 1559. The cylindrical body flares upwards, and the bottom section, marked off by moulding, is decorated with nielloed plant motifs.

15th-century domestic silver

With the exception of literary references, details in paintings, inventories, wills and scant museum holdings, little remains of the silver made for domestic use during the 15th century.

Wenzel Jamnitzer

Often called "the German Cellini," Wenzel Jamnitzer (1508-85) is universally recognized as the greatest German silversmith of all time. No more than twenty-five works have survived that can be definitely attributed to Jamnitzer, and all of them display such technical perfection and stylistic homogeneity that establishment of a chronological sequence is difficult. It would be pointless to make any further attributions without sound documentation, for they would have no validity given the artistic situation in 16th-century Nuremberg, where many talented artists worked (among them Jamnitzer's own brother, Albrecht), passing on their skills from father to son. Jamnitzer's works consist mainly of display pieces, many based on designs engraved by Peter Flötner and Virgil Solis, often executed for emperors and officials of the church and court. His works are characterized by careful proportions, abundant decoration often enriched by inlaid stones or other precious materials, statuettes of an elegant refinement, and the faithful reproduction of animals and plants, a common trait of Renaissance artists, who were fascinated by scientific studies.

During this period the arts in Europe followed two routes, the innovative movement of the Italian Renaissance and the lingering late Gothic, then reaching its most elaborate stage with the so-called flamboyant Gothic. In Italy, Siena and Florence became centers of the art of silverworking, for silver could be worked in sculptural forms in keeping with the Renaissance spirit, giving prevalence to the human figure; silver pieces from these Tuscan cities frequently reflect contemporary works of sculpture. The Tuscan influence spread to Rome, but in Venice, Genoa and Piedmont late Gothic models continued to prevail. In France, a wide variety of silver objects was made for

Right: Drinking horn in silver by Frederik Jans, Amsterdam, 1566. The base with its architectural structure is joined to the horn by a sculptural element in the shape of a dragon.

Below: Spoon in silver with gilt finial. England, c. 1400. The bowl is crescent shaped, and the stem is of hexagonal section.

head, mark); in 1363 a second mark, the maker's mark, was introduced; and in 1478 a year mark, consisting of a letter of the alphabet, was added (but the series of date letters began only in 1558). France adopted letters as year marks in 1460.

Silver in the German states

German 16th-century silver reflects two important factors: the enormous proliferation of decorative motifs and the activity of silversmiths of exceptional skill. During this period the flamboyant Gothic

the decoration of the festive table: ewers and basins, standing salts, a wide variety of beakers and cups, wine pitchers and handled bowls. The most curious object was the navicella, a silver piece shaped like a little ship that was placed on the table in front of guests; the top could be removed, and inside the cavity were a napkin, flatware and cup.

Silvermaking in German-speaking areas was widespread and impressive with a decorative repertory closely tied to the late Gothic style. The chief centers of production were in prosperous regions: free imperial cities like Augsburg,

Nuremberg and Strasbourg as well as the cities of the Hanseatic League, such as Hamburg, Danzig and Lübeck, the capital of overseas commercial trade. Among the most important objects were the double cups traditionally used in marriage ceremonies, drinking horns, horns mounted in silver and entirely covered with Gothic tracery, beakers and tankards. The Flemings preferred smooth surfaces entirely decorated with the technique of niello in arabesques and vines with intertwined human or animal figures. On the Iberian peninsula, Gothic motifs were mixed with the traditional motifs of Moorish culture. However, a large number of German, French and Flemish gold- and silversmiths were in Spain, and they contributed to the repertory of shapes and decorations. The system of hallmarks as guarantees of quality became more organized during this century. In 1300 King Edward I of England had ordered that silver be provided with a mark of guarantee (the king's, or leopard's

16TH CENTURY

Below left: Ewer in par-cel-gilt silver. Italy, c. 1560. Shaped like a vase with a highly pro-nounced spout with beaded border. The handle is shaped like a female figure with scrolls.

Below right: Tigerware jug with silver cover and fittings by John Jones, Exeter, c. 1575. The cover, hinged to the upper border, is embossed with lobes and foliate motifs.

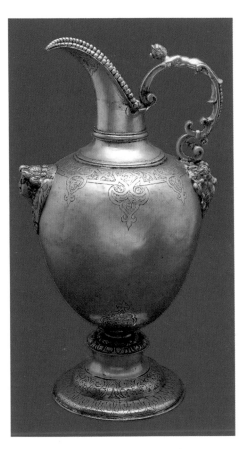

style gave way to an enthusiastic welcoming of Renaissance trends. The fact that Germans took the lead in European silver production during this period is without doubt a result of the presence of a great artist, whose creative genius was expressed in both gold- and silverworking: Albrecht Dürer (1471-1528). Dürer was an apprentice in his father's goldsmith workshop before dedicating himself to painting, and he later made many designs for impressive,

complex works in silver, including table fountains, progenitors of centerpieces, navicellas and covered cups. Another important artist who furnished designs for silversmiths was the medallist and craftsman Peter Flötner (1485-1546), whose woodcuts include decorations with flowers, vines, grotesques and classical swags and niches that are at least partly a result of his studies in Italy. He applied his fertile imagination to models based on Italian

Renaissance types to create the magnificent and over-loaded repertory of decoration typical of German silver of the period. Dürer and Flötner were not the only artists supplying designs for silver; many other German artists contributed new and stimulating designs that inspired the work of silversmiths. Among the many were Hans Sebald Beham (1500-50), painter and engraver; Virgil Solis (1514-62), miniaturist, painter and engraver; and Mathis Zündt

The Cassetta Farnese, made between 1548 and 1561 by Manno di Bastiano Sbarri for Cardinal Alexander Farnese, with six rock-crystal plaquettes by Giovanni Bernardi Castelbolognese.

(1498-1572), sculptor, engraver and goldsmith. An important contribution to German silver was made by the vast production of the celebrated Nuremberg artist Wenzel Jamnitzer (1508-85), leading member of a family of German goldsmiths and engravers, a dynasty renowned for splendid decoration, ingenious creations and high technical achievements. Among the most interesting works are a series of magnificently engraved cups without covers; cups with covers and flared bodies decorated with hammered scales or a diamond-pattern motif; and celebrated double cups composed of one cup that rests on a base with a cover formed by a smaller

16TH-CENTURY ORNAMENTAL MODELS

The decoration of silver during the 16th century was greatly influenced by the large-scale production of models for goldsmiths, which was based on a firmly established tradition in the countries of central Europe, particularly in the German-language areas. Many collections of designs were exported and came into widespread use; for example, the well-known series of Moresque designs published at Antwerp in 1557 by Balthasar van

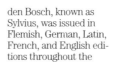

den Bosch, known as Sylvius, was issued in Flemish, German, Latin, French, and English editions throughout the second half of the 16th century and early 17th century, contributing to the enormous success of these motifs.

Bottom: Elephant with figures in gilt silver by Christoff Ritter, Nuremberg, c. 1570. The tower-shaped structure is removable and contains four armed men.

Opposite above: Cup in filigreed silver on a gilt background, Venice, 16th century. Cone-shaped with a flared base, this is finely decorated with motifs of vines and leaves.

cup. These double cups continue the decorative repertory of the late Gothic with the addition of elements in the Renaissance style. Of particular interest are apple- and pear-shaped cups mounted on high, plantform stems. Gigantic double cups with surfaces covered by a profusion of Renaissance motifs are characteristic of the production of the silversmith Theophil Glaubich of Augsburg. A particular kind of drinking vessel, popular in both the German and Flemish areas, was a type of cup shaped like an upside-down bell topped by a handle in the shape of a windmill or animal; such vessels had no base and were held in the hand when drinking wine. These curious objects are called *Stürzbecher*. An even stranger variant is the *Jungferbecher*, which consists of an upside-down chalice in the shape of a dress topped by a female bust with raised arms that hold a second, smaller cup on hinges. Such cups were used by a betrothed couple, who had to drink at the same time from the two chalices without spilling any wine, a difficult operation. The ewer

Engraving and chasing

Decorative techniques involving the use of pointed implements to incise patterns on a surface are as old as humankind, as indicated by the many examples of rock carvings made by primitive cultures. In the field of silver, such decoration involves tracing a design on the surface using a metal point. The tool used is a burin, which consists of a metallic cutting head attached to a wooden handle. By pressing with the hollow of the hand lines of varying thicknesses are created, the thickness depending on the amount of pressure exerted and on the angle of the burin in relation to the surface. The result is the permanent removal of tiny shavings of metal. From a technical point of view, there is no limit to the thinness of the grooves created using the burin. It is interesting to note that chiaroscuro effects can be achieved by creating a series of hatched or cross-hatched lines of varying density. The technique of engraving is often associated with that of chasing. This is achieved using small, blunt-ended metal chisels that, when struck with a hammer, have the effect of gently denting the surface of the silver without scratching it in order to emphasize the outline of shapes, to make sharp corners, and to give greater definition to modelling. Chisels are made in a wide variety of different types, and each craftsman assembles his own set so that the appropriate one is always at hand. The techniques of engraving and chasing metal, often associated with embossing, are called toreutics, from toreus, a Greek word for a boring tool.

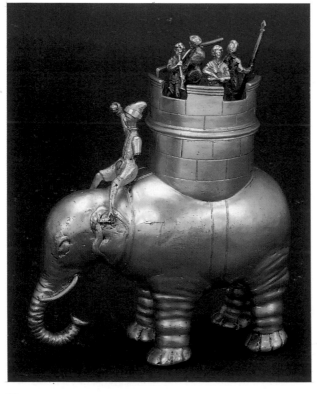

tapered beakers, the smooth bodies of which were covered with engraved decorations of Renaissance motifs.

Iberian silver

A love for silver within a decorative framework that completely covers the entire surface of the object is typical of the Iberian peninsula and reflects the *horror vacui* inspired on the one hand by long contact with Arab culture and on the other by the magnificence of late Italian Renaissance art. Without doubt, the most significant form was still the matched ewer and basin. The Portuguese preferred the representation of man in the wilderness, such as African and hunting scenes, while the Spanish were attracted to the triumphs derived from Italian art. The Spanish silver that shows the influence of the Italian sculptors and goldsmiths Leone Leoni (1509-90) and his son Pompeo (c. 1533-1608), both of whom served Charles V, displays a certain tendency

and basin were offered a wide range of expression by the decorative motifs of the Renaissance. The favoured themes were taken from classical mythology and history, such as the battle of the Titans, the myth of Orpheus, the rape of Europa and Roman triumphs.

Flemish silver

A singular object from this period is the drinking horn, composed of a cow horn mounted in an elaborate silver structure formed of a base fitted with supporting figures. These figures hold a ring into which the horn in inserted. Symbolic decoration runs around the outside of the ring and on the end and mouth of the horn. Such monumental objects were used by the corporations or

guilds of the various arts and crafts, the members of which would drink together from this symbolic drinking horn. In Holland works in silver were made in the form of animals, often birds of prey with fish held in their talons, while a popular form in the German area was an elephant bearing a tower full of warriors on its back. The skill of Flemish engravers found expression in slightly

to introduce fanciful motifs that betray their Gothic origins although within a context of clearly Renaissance forms.

Italian silver

The noblest examples of silver from 16th-century Italy are linked to the exceptional figure of Benvenuto Cellini (1500-71), sculptor, metalsmith and author of a celebrated autobiography, who created many monumental examples in which the influence of Michelangelo and of the entire artistic movement known as Mannerism is presented in models with a European resonance. There is, for example, the famous *Cassetta Farnese*, made by a pupil of Cellini's, which is of clear Michelangelesque inspiration in the statues and winged sphinxes, the mythological figures and hunting and battle scenes. The same can be said for Venetian works in filigree or with inlaid rock crystal, for the impressive Genoese ewers and basins, Sicilian embossed plates and the works of Lombard smiths.

French silver

The Italian influence on 16th-century French silver was a result of both the presence of Cellini at the court of Francis I and the models designed in France by Rosso Fiorentino (1494-1541). Even so, it was with the Fontainebleau school that French silver finally abandoned Gothic influences and followed the new style, adopting a decorative repertory that included acanthus leaves, vines, pilaster strips, capitals, mythological figures and forms taken from classical antiquity. Forms appear with continuous decoration, as in the case of ewers and basins, and objects such as pitchers were produced in basic forms that prefigure the simplicity of the early 17th century.

17TH-CENTURY SILVER

The early 17th century
The baroque

THE EARLY
17TH CENTURY

The growth of domestic silver

The enormous quantities of bullion that arrived in Europe from the Americas at the beginning of the 17th century had a profound effect on Europe's monetary systems, particularly on the silver used in minting coins. This abundance of raw materials also contributed to a vigorous growth in the arts of gold- and silver-smithing, both of which underwent increased production. Up to the end of the previous century objects in wrought plate were not just a sign of wealth but represented actual wealth, for they could be used, based on their weight, as a form of exchange that could be given or lent based on monetary value, which remained more or less constant. Now, however, the influx of large quantities of silver from the Americas caused fluctuations that no longer permitted financial operations based on objects. The only way to convert capital into cash was to melt down the objects and have them made into coins.

Although silver lost some of its mythical appeal, it acquired a new social role during this period: that of providing a sense of refinement and social status both in home furnishings and table settings. This role became increasingly important over time. Wealthy Europeans still displayed buffets of plate, sideboards on which silver plates, vases, pitchers, wine coolers and candelabra were displayed, perhaps together with porcelain from the Far East.

The development of silver production was undoubtedly favoured by the social and economic changes that resulted from increased mercantile activity and the strengthening of the landed aristocracy, for whom silver objects, especially those made for display, had always offered a means of hoarding wealth. The growth of secular silver also reflects social change, for European society was undergoing a renewal, with private homes that were increasingly inviting and castles that were decreasingly gloomy and dark. This brought with it new guidelines for polite society and a refinement of the art of entertainment. In the midst of this, objects of silver came to perform an important role in domestic rituals. As with the other applied arts, the development of secular silver took place within a radical transformation of forms, decorative repertories and styles. The regulations controlling the guilds of artisans and their numbers came under greater control, and silversmiths were increasingly taken into consideration. Proof of this is in the fact that when King Henry IV of

France decided to give space to artists by granting them the use of rooms in the gallery of the Louvre for their shop workers, he included areas for gold-and silversmiths.

Renaissance models and new forms

Various types of display plate were still being made during this transitional period, including standing mazers and elaborate cups. These imposing utensils continued the Renaissance tradition that began with Italian models, such as those in Florence's Museo degli Argenti in the Pitti

Bottom: Tazza with pedestal foot in gilt silver with chased and nielloed decoration, made in Spain, early 17th century. The oval body bears decorative motifs related to Renaissance models.

Below: Wine goblet with shaped stem and cone cup with engraved inscription and coat of arms made by the English silversmith Walter Shute and hallmarked London dating to 1627.

Palace. They were composed of a round (or, more rarely, elliptic) cup that was entirely embossed and chased with an allegorical, mythological or symbolic scene and was supported by a truncated cone, tapering cylinder or stem. During the early 17th century the central scene was replaced by a composition of decorative motifs taken from the repertory of current fashion. These were large leaves, rosettes and small heads, both male and female. The central scene was thus replaced by a decorative context that tended itself to become the protagonist of the object, and that was made possible by the exuberance of the stylistic elements of late Man-

nerism. This movement towards general decoration occurred in other areas of Europe, especially the Iberian peninsula, but in France and the German-speaking areas the central-scene model survived until around 1620.

Tableware: cups, tankards, spoons

The most interesting and prestigious object used in table settings of this period is the covered cup, or tankard. Closely tied to the traditions of German-speaking countries (and known originally as "hans cups" in England), covered cups were a status symbol, with their use generally restricted to the rich, to the master

THE EARLY
17TH CENTURY

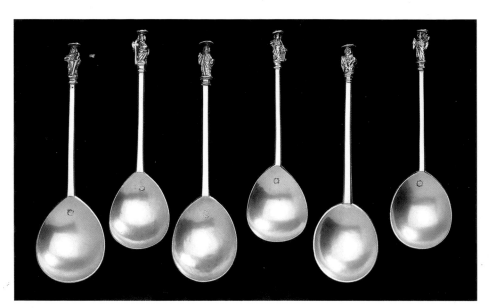

of the house or his important guests. The shape of this silver object is related to late 15th- and 16th-century models in which Gothic stylistic elements were prevalent. During the early 17th century, the decoration became more simplified and the forms more basic, so much so that in some cases the cover takes the form of a small inverted cup. It is possible that this object, slowly increasing in size over time, finally became the common dedicatory or triumphal cup still very much alive in today's world of sports. In England during this period, wine goblets were made that were nothing more than the translation into silver of glass containers. The form is therefore based on a smooth chalice, suitable for dedica-

APOSTLE SPOONS

Apostle spoons, so-named for their finials decorated in the shape of the apostles, were made during the late 15th century but became widespread in England during the 16th. The complete set generally comprised thirteen spoons, with the twelve apostles and Christ, or "the Master"; complete sets are rare today, in part because they were a standard christening gift, whether singly or in sets. The bowls of early examples were pear-shaped, but in the course of the 17th century they became progressively more oval and deeper. The stem was generally of hexagonal section, but over the course of time stems grew longer and, in particular after circa 1660, began to appear in oval section. The finials were cast separately and then soldered to the spoon

St. Matthew

St. James the Great

St. Jude (Thaddaeus)

St. Mathias

St. Andrew

St. Simon

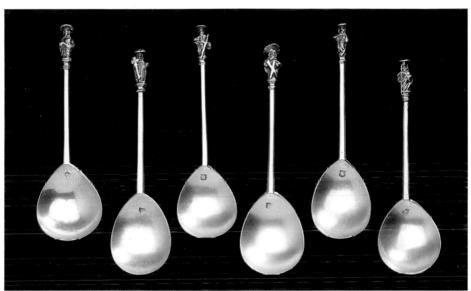

tory inscriptions or family armorials, mounted on a well-turned, elegant foot. The most important object of English tableware during this period was the spoon, most of which had deep oval bowls and straight handles ending in a finial. This object of extraordinary simplicity, elegance and harmonious proportions ranks among the leading examples of design. The decoration of the finial at the end of the handle served to balance the weight of the bowl, making the spoon easier to use. Spoons were often used as christening gifts, and engraved initials often appear on the bowl or back. The tankard underwent large development in England. As in the German-speaking world, it was an emblematic object, a sym-

and were often gilt. The saints can be identified according to their characteristic attributes: St. Matthew with the axe; St. James the Great with the pilgrim's staff: St. Jude (Thaddaeus) with the cudgel; St. Andrew with the decussate cross; St. Simon with the saw; St. James the Less with the club; St. Philip with stones; St. Bartholomew with the large knife;

St. James the Less

St. Philip

St. Bartholomew

St. Thomas

St. John

St. Peter

St. Thomas with the lance; St. John in the act of blessing; and St. Peter with the key. St. Mathias is difficult to recognize, in part because he is so little known. St. Paul, often considered an apostle although not among the twelve followers of Christ, is sometimes included. Initials are often engraved on the bowl or back of the bowl of apostle spoons.

THE EARLY
17TH CENTURY

bolic piece usually reserved for the master of the house, and its decoration, the value of the material it was made from, as well as the refinement of the craftsmanship served the function of delivering a message to guests: they communicated the financial standing of its owner. A compact shape, heavy base and large or heavy handle are aspects that contributed to defining its importance. In some cases, the solid base was replaced by three feet in the shape of a ball or a lion holding a ball between its front paws. Tankards were made in England, the Low Countries and the German-

speaking areas. In most cases the central body of the tankard is embossed and chased both with figurations and geometric motifs; however, tankards were also made with smooth bodies (these were favoured in Denmark and Sweden), and some were decorated with silver coins. This type of decoration, already in use during the preceding century, can be found on a tankard that dates from 1540 and is preserved at the Bayerische Nationalmuseum of Munich; 36 ancient Roman silver coins are inserted in its surface. Without doubt the combination of wrought silver and silver coins reveals the owner's desire for the ostentatious display of wealth.

Opposite above:
Tankard in gilt silver by
the Augsburg goldsmith
Johan Flicker III. The
entire surface bears
relief and chased
decoration in a dia-
mond-face motif.

Opposite bottom:
Tankard in gilt silver
with maker's mark of
Esaias Zur Linden,
Nuremberg, first quar-
ter 17th century. The
body is finely chased
with hexagonal motifs.

Below: Large (51 cm
high) tankard made
in Zwickau, c. 1684.
Applied to the surface
of the body are 94 coins,
with 5 more inserted
on the top of the cover.

The tankard

*The tankard is a particular
sort of large drinking cup used
primarily in countries where
beer is the usual drink. The
name is derived from a Persian
word meaning "cistern," a
reflection of the tankard's large
capacity. Tankards are usually tall cylinders with a single
handle and hinged cover with
a thumbpiece with which the
cover can be easily raised by
the hand holding the tankard.
These containers have been
made of pewter, crystal and
also porcelain, in which case
the cover is separate. Silver
tankards are valuable because
of the material used and are
also practical because silver
keeps beer cool. The bodies of
tankards were originally of
two basic types: the popular
tapering cylindrical variety
and a rarer pear-shaped type.
The base is of various types; it
is most often circular with
moulding, but rare examples
stand on three spheres or small
feet. The bodies of many
tankards are completely
smooth, others are decorated
with engraved and chased
motifs, and in some cases the
body and cover are sumptu-
ously embossed and chased. In
the case of tankards made as
presentation gifts, the decoration usually includes an
engraved dedication. In
German areas silver coins were
often added to the body of
tankards as decoration. In such
cases the body of the piece is
usually quite high to make
room for more coins. The interiors of tankards were often gilt to
improve the flavour of the beer.*

The persistence of Renaissance models and the first simple forms

During the first thirty years
of the 17th century the
Renaissance motifs that
formed the traditional repertory remained strong, particularly in terms of display
plate. Chief among these
were the nautiluses, which
offered silversmiths the
opportunity to express themselves in imaginative displays that were always, however, based on stylistic
elements from late Man-
nerism. During the same
period works in silver
appeared that were virtually
without decoration. Covered
beakers and pitchers ap-
peared in essential forms.
One must be cautious when
dating silver from this period
on the basis of style alone;
English silver was fiercely
conservative, tending to
repeat styles of the past. The
political events that were
troubling Europe at this time
also had an influence on the
type of silver objects being

27

THE EARLY 17TH CENTURY

created. The crisis of the English monarchy, the decline of Spain, the war between Spain and Holland, the religious problems in France: these events may have caused a decline in wealth and resulted in demand for simple, clean and essential forms, less decorated and therefore less expensive, alongside the over-decorated.

Strict controls of silverworking

Since the relationship between silver and coin money was so close, governments took a close interest in the quality of silver used, sought to maintain a high standard of workmanship and collected taxes relating to the activities of silversmiths. The value and loca-

The nautilus

Mounted nautilus shells represent a curious period of silver. The distinctive shape of these shells was used with elaborate silver mounts, often gilt, to create bizarre luxury items. The nautilus, a cephalopod mollusk from the sole surviving genus of a subclass that flourished 200 million years ago, has a large spiralling coiled shell. This shape, called the spira mirabilis, *is, in fact, a logarithmic spiral. Nautiluses are found in the deep waters of the Indian and Pacific oceans. The shells arrived in Europe when the merchants of the various East India companies began bringing merchandise directly to Dutch ports and to those of the Hanseatic League. This explains why most silver-mounted nautiluses come from Germany and the Low Countries. The form of the shell and its spirals were integrated in the mountings to create almost surreal forms, sometimes becoming the body of a naiad, dragon, or sea monster. Such works often include the figure of Neptune riding a dolphin. These silver objects, which gave connoisseurs an opportunity to show off their wealth and refined taste, are a manifestation of the high baroque that sometimes reaches almost excessive levels of virtuosity. The great popularity of mounted nautilus shells is indicated by many painting of sumptuous interiors in which these large pieces stand out as the central elements in arrangements of other precious articles of display plate.*

Left: Cup and cover by the silversmith Georg Winckler hallmarked in Augsburg, 1696. The finial is the symbol of Augsburg, and the piece is decorated with engravings of 18 coats of arms and names.

Bottom: Ewer with cylindrical body with engraved coat of arms, scroll handle, and beak-shaped spout. The base is a reversed cone. Made in London, 1664.

the work was submitted to a quality control performed by the guild of silversmiths to which the smith belonged. The assayer's hallmark and the other test hallmarks changed every two years, so by reading the marks it is possible to establish the period during which an object of silver was made, and an examination of the silversmith's hallmark will reveal the name of the maker.

An equally scrupulous system of hallmarks came to be adopted in England, where the use of hallmarks with date letters permits easy identification of the exact year of production; other hallmarks give the quality of silver, the place of production and name of the silversmith.

In Mediterranean countries, the standard of silver was established in "deniers." The measure is divided into 12 deniers, and the denier into 24 grains. Therefore silver of 11 deniers is equal to 916.6/1000, that of 10 deniers is 833.3, and so on. In German-speaking countries the unit is divided in *lötiges* and the *lotig* in 18 grains; 16 *lötiges* are equal to 1,000 parts fine silver (100 per cent silver), and 14.8 *lötiges* are equal to 925 parts fine silver (92.5 per cent fine silver, the same as the English sterling standard). In the British Isles two standards were used: "sterling standard," equal to 925/1000, and Britannia standard, equal to 958.3/1000.

tion of silver pieces was also monitored, to impose, if necessary, their restitution to the state in order to provide material for coins.

An example of this government involvement is the strict system adopted in France in the area of Paris. When a piece of silver had been roughly shaped, the silversmith marked it with his personal hallmark and submitted it to a first examination by a state-contracted tax examiner, who marked the piece with an assay hallmark. When the piece was completed it was again tested, and the silversmith paid a tax; it was then marked with a hallmark indicating it was "free" of charges. Finally

THE BAROQUE

Social reflections in baroque silver

Political events in three areas of Europe had important effects on silver production: the coming to power in France of King Louis XIV (1661); the Commonwealth, Protectorate and restoration of the monarchy with Charles II in Great Britain (1649-60); and the expansion of power and cultural golden age of the Netherlands. Louis XIV tried to bring about a profound transformation of French society, one that would affirm both the absolute rule of the centralized state over every aspect of the country's life as well as the nation's hegemony in Europe. This political absolutism tended of necessity to translate itself into intellectual absolutism: the arts and culture in general were considered instruments of power comparable to military or economic might. With the aid of his minister Jean Baptiste Colbert (1619-83) and the painter, decorator and architect Charles Le Brun (1619-90), the reign of Louis XIV was

17TH-CENTURY DECORATIVE MOTIFS
A great deal of 17th-century silver was influenced by the many books of patterns printed in different countries, which led to a certain uniformity in style. Even so, some production areas developed independent and original themes and languages. Italian silversmiths, for example, remained faithful to late-Renaissance motifs, which slowly evolved towards a typically baroque expression, although in Italy the baroque did not reach the exuberance shown elsewhere. The style was influenced by models by Laurenziani, Scoppa, Bernini, Ferri and Cerini and was expressed using such traditional motifs as scrolls, festoons, rib-

bons, acanthus leaves, cartouches, beading, gadrooning and anthropomorphic or angelic figures.

one in which the king was universally recognized as the absolute ruler. This new style, an eclectic and imposing classicism, was expressed in silver produced on the vastest scale ever seen, which reached its height in the period 1660-90. Court silver included objects of every type, from table services to chandeliers and even furniture. The political, military and economic problems caused by the many wars of the period forced the king to order the melting down of almost all the nation's silver through a series of edicts issued incessantly from 1688 to 1709. Few pieces from the period have survived. In England, the period of the Commonwealth was beset by economic difficulties related to the struggles for power between the parliamentarians and the royalists who

The great interest in scientific matters also influenced decoration; nature became a great source of inspiration, particularly during the second half of the century, when the interpretation of plant and animal subjects became constant, reflected most of all in motifs of floral design, which were popular in France as well as in Italy. In the second half of the 17th century, the close involvement of monarchs in every artistic expres- sion led to a revitalization of silver, which was employed to express the "grandeur" of court; thus it is often overdecorated with the austere motifs of classical inspiration typical of the Louis XIV style: vases with large bunches of flowers, large shells, allegorical figures and puttos, all rigidly symmetrical and somewhat heavy.

longed for the return of the king. Money was needed to pay soldiers, so silver was melted down. The few works made are of an exemplary simplicity, undoubtedly a result of financial restrictions as well as the Puritan disdain for ornate decoration. The restoration of the monarchy in 1660 brought a return to sumptuous silver, with pieces decorated in a profusion of motifs, often made using the techniques of embossing and engraving and showing clear baroque tendencies, as well as a wide variety of other models, made in great numbers in part because of the return of royal patronage.

Around the end of the century, the coronation of Prince William of Orange and Mary as joint rulers brought Dutch and French influence to English silver,

for William had employed French artists in Holland and brought some of these, as well as Dutch artisans, with him to England.

The Peace of Westphalia, which ended the Thirty Years' War in 1648, also brought about recognition of the independence of the United Provinces—as the independent Netherlands was called—which was by

then the greatest sea power in Europe. The mercantile activities of the Dutch East and West India companies supported a wealthy and enlightened middle class for whom abundant silver vessels were the outward symbol of a comfortable life. Dutch silversmiths also had the advantage of contributions from Huguenots, French Calvinists who fled persecution in France and took advantage of the religious tolerance in the Netherlands, bringing with them their artistic skills and contributing to the nation's prosperity.

Decoration in Italy

Italian silver of this period makes frequent reference to the great sculptural tradition of the baroque. The use of cast pieces—veritable silver sculptures—was common, especially for religious silver. Although religious pieces are beyond the

scope of this book, Italian ones dating from this period must be mentioned because they made use of all the stylistic traits of the time: inflated and imposing forms in which modelled areas are heavily emphasized; curls and broad spirals; a cautious re-interpretation of models taken from the last period of classical antiquity. All this contributes to forms whose visual impact is one of dynamic movement and power. Little domestic silver has survived, and since Italy was then divided into various states, there were many production centers. Among the most famous were those of Venice, Genoa, Florence, Rome, Messina and Turin.

Decoration in France

The decoration of silver, in particular that used at court, was carefully codified in France by the publication of many pattern books used by silversmiths as reference works. The basic concept was an extreme fidelity to symmetry in motifs. These motifs were based on foliate scrolls, seashells, small heads (both male and female), garlands of flowers and fruit, compact palm leaves, scrolled acanthus leaves, and borders decorated with a motif known as the bean motif (originally from Holland) and gadrooning. Gadrooning came to be among the motifs favoured for the decoration of curved

THE DECORATION OF HANDLES
The possession and use of silver were long prerogatives of a few privileged classes; thus, aside from any specific function, works in silver were often symbols of the social status and wealth of their owner, and as such they had considerable communicative value. This value was often represented by decorative abundance, precise execution, and attention to the smallest detail. Even those elements with precise functional uses, such as the handles of cups, ewers, tankards, or porringers, were shaped with great attention and were often elaborately decorated. The types of handle most common in the 17th century were those in the shape of an S or reversed S; the most common decorative motifs were foliate scrolls and beading or those based on zoomorphic or anthropomorphic forms.

THE BAROQUE

areas of silver and was used for three centuries throughout the world.

Decoration in England

Two motifs were favoured early in this period: hunting scenes with dogs, deer, boars, stags, hunters and motifs of broad-surfaced flowers and leaves. The leaves became gradually smaller and more detailed and the foliate scroll, used in particular for the handles of caudle cups (two-handled cups used for hot drinks), became a leading motif. The lion's head began to assume its enduring importance as a traditional English motif. Also traditionally English is engraved decoration, especially on salvers or on the smooth areas of cups, where coats of arms appear within typically baroque frames. This period saw the triumph of the intricately spiralled cartouche. Motifs taken from the Louis XIV style began to spread around the end of the century, but in simplified, more restrained, versions. This is understandable given the presence in England of skilled Huguenot silversmiths. The Huguenots had long suffered religious persecution in France and had fled, primarily to the Netherlands but also to England. Henry IV had supposedly ended this persecution with the Edict of Nantes in 1598, but its provisions were gradually eroded until, in 1685, Louis XIV revoked it altogether, leading to the arrival in England of thousands of Huguenots, many of whom thus found themselves in England after a period in the Netherlands. One of the leading silver designers of the period, Daniel Marot (1663-1752), fled first to Holland, where he contributed to the diffusion of the Louis XIV style. He became architect to William of Orange and accompanied him when he took the throne of England in 1688. Three artistic tendencies can be said to have co-existed in England during this period: that based

Chinoiserie

Chinoiserie refers to decorations inspired by Oriental models used on Western objects. Chinoiserie are never exact copies of models from the Far East, but are always interpretations of those motifs. The European craftsmen ignored the symbolism connected to those ornaments, but the same can be said of the other aspects of Oriental arts assimilated in Europe. The first examples of chinoiserie were designs for silver made by the Dutch engraver Mathias Beitler in 1616, later joined by the vast series of "Chinese-style" models published by De Moedler in 1694. Throughout the 17th century the chinoiserie decoration of silver was based on the decoration of Oriental lacquers and porcelain. In most cases, the shape of the piece maintains its European appearance, and only the decoration is exotic. The favoured themes were fantastic birds, phoenixes, dragons and Oriental figures and architecture, almost always engraved. This engraved decoration was in use until about 1740, after which sculptural decoration became more frequent; the techniques used tended increasingly towards embossing and chasing to create relief decoration. The examples are of a high quality of workmanship and show a mixture of rococo stylistic elements with those of the Far East. This decoration is clearly a free interpretation of Oriental decorative motifs. Not infrequently the chinoiserie reflects suggestions from painters like Watteau, Lancret and Pillement.

on Restoration style; that introduced by the Huguenot silversmiths; and finally the Queen Anne style, which was marked by austere simplicity and essential forms and was used primarily for domestic plate.

Silver for lighting

Various forms of candlesticks were in wide use. These include simple candlesticks with a socket for a candle; branched candlesticks, or candelabra, with several sockets; and chandeliers, branched fixtures made to be suspended from the ceiling. The candelabra of this period usually have a wide base with somewhat swollen motifs, a stem with pronounced gadrooning, a fairly small candle holder and an equally small plate beneath to catch wax. Candelabra were usually made in pairs; the style for four-piece sets began only towards the end of the century. Examples of silver chandeliers are rare and are found in two typical models: the Louis XIV style, with large, flowing decoration in baroque swirls, and the style commonly called Dutch,

THE BAROQUE

Ewer made in Messina, 17th century. Attached to the vase-shaped body decorated with chasing are a spout shaped like a mask with curls and scrolls and a handle that ends in a lion's head.

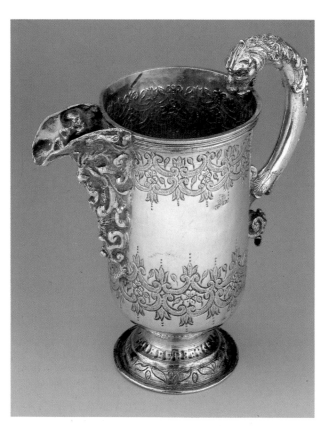

spread in France and Italy. Italian silversmiths also made a certain number of elegant bed warmers and basins. The late baroque decoration of such pieces is delicate and light, particularly those made in Venice.

Flatware of the 17th century

Throughout the 17th century changes were made to flatware that eventually led to an evolution that was both formal and related to the more delicate aspects of function and custom. The varieties of types multiplied, as did the decorative creativity and the use of materials; however, the multitude of materials used in the Renaissance period gradually diminished, and the recourse to silver became increasingly persistent, most of all for use in the great halls of royal courts. It was during the 17th century that the custom of the *couvert*—the place setting of matched flatware arranged before each diner—came into use. This custom presented the need for knives, forks and spoons made following the same decorative model. Until then each guest usually brought his or her own personal flatware, enclosed in a small case; the table service offered was just one or two knives, sometimes a spoon, and a toothpick. The fork took hold very slowly and in different ways;

characterized by a series of connected spheres.

Table silver

Typical of this period, especially in England, are containers for drinks and food, such as caudle cups, usually with two handles and a cover with finial, and porringers, also with two handles (such cups are also variously called posset cups and bleeding bowls). There were also punch bowls and monteiths. Monteiths are large bowls resembling punch bowls with a notched

rim used to suspend glasses in cool water. Other large table pieces included wine cisterns and wine coolers, or ice pails. Ewers and basins for the rinsing of hands were still being made (although the increasing use of the fork was leading to a decline in their use). These almost always bear striking decoration—sculptural handles and spouts adorned with human heads or those of wild beasts—for the type permitted silversmiths to give free rein to their imagination. Ewers and basins were also wide-

Bed warmers

Used for many centuries to combat the chill of winters in unheated homes, bed warmers have a long tradition. They usually consist of a covered pan made of iron, copper, brass, or, for the well to do, silver; in most cases they are round and flattened. They were made to hold hot coals, so the cover, almost always hinged and pierced, served the dual function of letting air enter the pan to keep the coals burning while at the same time protecting the bed sheets from fire. A wooden handle was usually attached to the side, often inserted in a fitting. The inside of silver bed warmers was made of iron to hold the coals; the outside surfaces were well suited to embossed decoration and, with the piercing of the cover, offered the silversmith an opportunity to indulge in fanciful decorative motifs. The piercing of the cover is the element of greatest prestige since is was based on pleasing harmony.

although in general use in Italy during the 16th century, it was not used and was indeed viewed with suspicion in other European countries, where pieces of food were stabbed with knife points and thus brought to the mouth. The earliest forks seem to have had only two prongs and were used primarily to hold meat when cutting.

A new way of holding flatware, using three fingers instead of the entire hand, gradually came into fashion; this new custom made the smooth or polygonal handles once prevalent obsolete and led to the development of flatter, longer stems.

The increasing use of the fork also meant the demise of sharp points on knives, which were no longer needed and were replaced by longer blades with rounded ends. Knife handles were made in a variety of shapes until, towards the end of the century, the "pistol" type began to prevail, destined to enjoy great popularity in the next period.

Until this period the spoon and fork had little in common in terms of form but they now began a stylistic reconciliation, the handles of both evolving from variously shaped grips into longer, flatter stems with a rectangular section. The end of the handle was often engraved with a coat of arms, and around the middle of the century the so-called trifid spoons, in

THE BAROQUE

which the end has a slight three-lobed shape reminiscent of small leaves, became popular in Great Britain and France. The bowls of spoons became increasingly oval, with the widest area near the stem, and the attachment between the bowl and stem was often reinforced by rat tails, an extension of moulding beneath the bowl, either smooth or decorated.

Table forks assumed their definite form only towards the end of the century.

Since they were used to hold food and bring it to the mouth (instead of using a knife), the number of prongs increased to three and even four, curved slightly upwards the better to serve this new function.

THE SILVERSMITHS OF BOSTON

In the period between the mid 17th century and the first decades of the 18th century, the city of Boston became one of the most important centers of silver production in England's North American colonies. Much of the credit for this goes to John Hull (1624-83), an English goldsmith who emigrated to America around 1634 and opened a shop, working first with his

John Hull   Hull and Sanderson   Jeremiah Dummer

John Coney   Robert Sanderson

brother and then in partnership with Robert Sanderson (1608-93), also from London. (The two also minted coins, albeit illegally, for

Massachusetts in 1652.) Several silversmiths trained in his shop, first among them Jeremiah Dummer (1645-1718), credited with

introducing gadrooning to the United States (circa 1680), and John Coney (1656-1722), who made excellent table services and harmoniously combined the traditional types of English silver with gadrooning and fluting to create innovative and original works. The shops of these masters formed the next generation of silversmiths, led by John Edwards and John Allen.

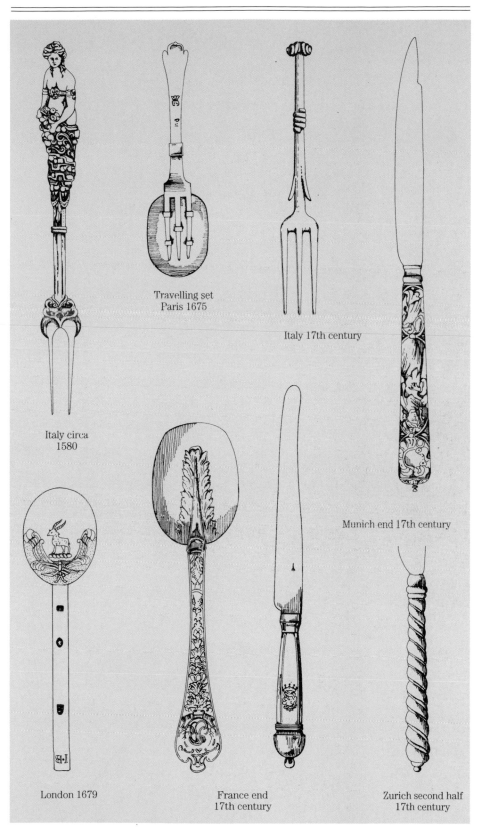

Travelling set
Paris 1675

Italy 17th century

Italy circa
1580

Munich end 17th century

London 1679

France end
17th century

Zurich second half
17th century

VARIOUS 17TH-CENTURY HALLMARKS

German-language countries

ZURICH	VIENNA	HAMBURG	NUREMBERG	LÜBECK

| 1621 | 17th cent. | 1699 | 17th cent. | from 16th to 18th cent. | 1631 |

AUGSBURG	CONSTANCE	MUNICH	BERLIN	FRANKFURT

| early 17th cent. mid 17th cent. | early 17th cent. | end 17th cent. | end 17th cent. | 17th cent. |

DÜSSELDORF	COLOGNE	LEIPZIG	BRUNSWICK	KASSEL	DRESDEN

| 17th cent. | end 17th cent. | 17th cent. | 17th cent. | 17th cent. | 17th cent. |

Low Countries

AMSTERDAM	HAARLEM	ANTWERP	BRUSSELS	TOURNAI

| 1655 | 17th cent. | 1644-45 | 1698-99 | 1635 | 1681 | 1626 | 1644 |

Italy

NAPLES	VENICE	ROME	LUCCA

| 17th cent. | end 17th early 18th cent. | end 17th cent. | end 16th early 17th cent. |

Iberian Peninsula

LISBON	OPORTO	TOLEDO	BARCELONA	ÁVILA

| end 17th early 18th cent. | 17th cent. | 1600 | 17th cent. | 17th cent. | end 17th early 18th cent. |

Great Britain

LONDON	YORK	NEWCASTLE	EXETER	GLASBOW	EDINBURGH

| from 1647 | from 1655 | from 1631 | from 1672 | from 1685 | from 1635 | from 1690 | from 1683 | from 1682 |

18TH-CENTURY SILVER

The early 18th century
Rococo
Neoclassicism

EARLY 18TH CENTURY

time, the classical and immutable ideal expressed in the stately court style was submitted to re-evaluation. Art became more human and spurned the grandiose and heroic to embrace the graceful, with themes reflecting life's charm. Its public as well as

Historical-cultural events and silver production

The first decades of the 18th century witnessed both the large-scale destruction of display plate as a result of sumptuary laws and the development of a new style that arose in reaction to the baroque and which would finally lead to the rococo. This movement began in France following the death, in 1715, of Louis XIV and the reassertion of the aristocracy's influence. This is the period of the so-called Régence style, a term that refers to the eight years of the regency of Philippe II, duc d'Orléans (1715-23),

but that is given a wider application that encompasses the period of transition in architecture and decoration between Louis XIV style and the rococo. In this sense, the period is taken to run from the beginning of the century until 1730. This process of transformation coincided with the growing weakness and consequent loss of prestige of the absolute monarch. The court moved from Versailles back to Paris, which meant, in effect, that the court ceased to exist: it was spread among the salons, drawing rooms and private circles that had been at the root of its 17th-century beginnings. At the same

Filigree

The decorative technique of filigree consists in bending or intertwining thin filaments of silver and attaching them at points of contact to a body. The silver filaments can be simple, meaning smooth, or "pearled," meaning composed of a series of tiny spheres or grains. The silver filaments are made using a drawplate with holes of various shape and size to suit the needs of the silversmith. Filigree can be applied directly to the smooth surface of an object or it can be made into openwork forms (separate and independent of the surface) that are then placed around the structure of the object; this latter method is called á jour mounting. Known since antiquity, filigree was used throughout Europe in the Middle Ages. The leading Italian centers of production were Venice, where it was given the proprietary name opus veneticum ad filum, and Genoa, and it was used in almost all the countries of the Islamic world. In the last century it found great favour in Spain, Holland and southern Germany and it is still in use. When buying a work with filigree it is best to make certain the filaments are silver and not plated copper.

its patrons were no longer what they had been under Louis XIV; the place of the court and state was taken by the aristocracy and urban middle class. Shapes and decoration changed with great fluidity during the Régence period and as a result the style has no easily identifiable character, presenting instead all the traits common to a style in transition and in search of identity. Located between the diametrically opposed poles of the late baroque (characterized as stately, asymmetrical and stylized) and the rococo (characterized by movement, asymmetry and naturalism), the Régence style clearly marks the various

stages in the evolution from baroque to rococo, at the same time managing to remain distinct from both. It must be pointed out also that no fewer than forty sumptuary laws and edicts, limiting extravagance in luxury, had been decreed for various reasons during the preceding period and had led to the melting down of much silver, particularly ornate display plate.

The melting down of this silver had obvious disastrous consequences, but the sumptuary laws made an important contribution to the evolution of silver. Some edicts, limiting the weight of silver pieces and prohibiting excessive exuberance in decoration,

favoured restraint and without doubt increased the quest for elegance. This was a period of great and rapid social change. The new social class, composed of the rich bourgeois businessmen and financiers, came to own works in silver that in the preceding century would have been restricted to just a few high-ranking people.

English silver, which was manufactured in enormous quantities, received a further stimulus during the period immediately following the Peace of Utrecht (1713), which augmented Britain's overseas possessions, soon to give Britain the world's greatest empire. The strength of the middle class in England grew as a result. During the reign of George I (1714-27), the Whig party followed doctrines in support of aristocratic large landholders and the interests of wealthy merchants.

The Triple Alliance signed by Great Britain, France and the Netherlands (1717), which became the Quadruple Alliance with the addition of the Holy Roman emperor (1718), led to a period of relative prosperity marked by the first movements towards agrarian and industrial capitalism. The nascent textile and metallurgical industries created new wealth. This economic situation enabled the English to

43

devote more energies to the pleasures of home and to the rites of entertainment, with a subdued luxury that involved a demand for domestic silver, which came to be characteristic of the traditional furnishings of the English home. In the area of today's Germany, despite the hardships brought on by continuous conflicts, including the wars of Polish Succession (1733-35) and Austrian Succession (1740-48), Prussia was beginning its hegemony, bringing a consequent refinement of court life in the various states as well as in the mercantile middle class, appearing there as elsewhere in Europe. Both princes and the rich middle class created an increasing demand for large quantities of silver, both tableware and pieces for daily use, such as toilet services and desk sets. Venice can be taken as characteristic of the situation in Italy. The city experienced a marked economic decline in terms of maritime commerce. The money accumulated in preceding centuries could no longer be reinvested in mercantile enterprises and was spent, instead, on fine living and luxuries.

Domestic English silver

A considerable quantity of domestic plate was made and used in English homes during this period. It is important to remember that silver was not only the prerogative of aristocratic homes, but was also to be found in those of the landed nobility and the urban middle class. Many items were made, most of them used to decorate the dining room. Among the various models was the Scottish shallow drinking vessel with ears for use as handles commonly known as the quaich. The shapes of these were quite simple,

CUT-CARD DECORATION

First developed during the second half of the 17th century, the technique of cut-card work was extensively applied in the decoration of silver in the first quarter of the 18th century. The process involves cutting strips of silver into a pattern and then soldering the strips to the body of an object. This soldering required considerable skill since the two parts had to

adhere perfectly, but the effect obtained was more precise than could be achieved by embossing. Cut-card decorations were used in particular for the

bases of tureens, cups and beakers, for the finishing of the fittings of handles to teapots and coffeepots, and for embellishing castors or covers. The body

of the work was often opacified to create an effect of contrast of light and colour with the applied motifs, which were made shinier through burnishing.

Opposite: Pair of fruit baskets made in London in 1703 by John Eckfourd. These oval, two-handled baskets are pierced and chased to imitate wickerwork.

Bottom: Oval salver with scalloped border chased with stylized foliate motifs. A family coat of arms is engraved in the center with rocailles encircling two crowned eagles.

Below: Punch bowl decorated with cartouches, armorial bearings, and masks. The ringed handles hang from masks of grotesque animal heads. Made in 1703 by the London silversmith William Denny.

and they were smooth-sided with a circular base. The decoration was minimal, usually chasing along the outside of the cup and along the outside of the handles. The largest and most prestigious table pieces were the traditional ones: punch bowls, monteiths, urns, wine coolers, ewers and basins, salvers and baskets. The shape and decoration of punch bowls often share certain stylistic similarities. The body is decorated with vertical chased gadroons or convex flutes that lighten the globular form and are broken by a cartouche enclosing an engraved armorial. The motifs of these cartouches, based on scrolls and fringed acanthus leaves, can be taken as representative of early 18th-century taste. Also commonly encountered are lion's heads used as masks

to hold the drop-ring handles on the sides. The upper lip of such punch bowls is usually scalloped to hold glasses; this scalloped border is often detachable. In the simpler examples, the body of the bowl is smooth and decorated with light chasing; these are often without the

detachable border, and instead the bowl's rim is itself scalloped or indented. The sole concession to relief decoration on such pieces are the lion's-head masks holding the drop rings. The decoration is more elaborate on such pieces as soup tureens. This decoration is usually presented discreetly on a bulbous body, especially the lower part, while the side handles and cover have heavier and more elaborate decoration. Particular attention was given to the handles, the heavy scrolling decoration of which is offset and softened by subtle foliate branching and also by the cover with its finial and chased decorations that often include floral and plant motifs in a cautious prelude to the rococo repertory. The custom of drinking chilled wine led to

45

the diffusion of ice buckets, wine coolers and wine cisterns. The decoration on wine cisterns usually begins with swollen gadrooning at the bottom of the elliptical body of the basin and moves on to applications of interwoven scrolls and heads alternating with seashells or palmettes. These objects also display the great interest in richly decorative sculptural forms, most clearly

evident in the large handles, often in the shape of dolphins, scrolls ending in lion heads, winged female busts, horses and anthropomorphic figures. No important changes were made to the shape of the ewer and basin, which remained similar to those of past centuries, but the decorations used underwent a notable transformation, and the body of the ewer became increasingly

simple. Here, too, the most easily recognizable element is the handle, usually impressively sculptural with a scroll handle or a handle in the shape of a female figure. The body of the ewer is usually smooth above, with decoration in vertical elements concentrated towards the bottom, thus giving the form a pleasing sense of movement. The border of the rim of the basin is often

EARLY 18TH-CENTURY DECORATIVE MOTIFS
From the stylistic point of view, the first thirty years of the 18th century were a period of transition marking the passage from the baroque to the rococo. Particularly in France, this transitional style took on a well-defined form, although it displays the clear signs of being a period of formal research still in progress. Although definable and recognizable, the decorative repertories of the Régence style present all

the characteristics of this passage from the themes typical of the Louis XIV style to those, in certain senses diametrically opposed, that

prevailed in the Louis XV period. Ornamental motifs were still presented in a symmetrical layout, although somewhat less rigid, and they

were still pervaded by a pronounced tendency towards stylization; references to nature became more constant, and the whole seems

Opposite left: Tray with three feet marked with a Milan hallmark and dating to the first years of the 18th century. The smooth surface is framed by a layered moulding.

Opposite right: Silver vase made in Venice and datable to between the 17th and 18th century. The base and central section are decorated with large, embossed bean motifs.

Below: Large (maximum width 84.7 cm) wine cistern made by the London silversmith Jacob Margas in 1714. The upper border bears gadrooning, and the body is decorated with applied decorations

decorated with the elements typical of the period's taste: scrolls, seashells and the fringe-like ornaments called lambrequins.

Britannia standard

Between the end of the 17th century and the first years of the 18th, a variation occurred in the hallmarking designating the silver standard of wrought plate in Great Britain. Since 1545 the lion passant hallmark, showing a lion in full profile walking left, had been used to indicate the standard of silver, known as the sterling standard, which was 92.5 per cent fine silver. In 1697 King William III decided to impose a higher standard of purity, bringing it to 95.84 per cent. This change was due to the needs to curb the widespread habit of melting down silver coins or coin-clipping (trimming silver from the edges of coins) in order to re-use the metal in the production of silver. This practice had come to affect the number of coins in circulation, forcing the mint to make new ones. The scarcity of coins in circulation was adversely affecting the economy and a remedy was needed. Thus in 1697 the lion passant was replaced by a hallmark showing the figure of Britannia, a seated woman with helmet, lance and shield. The new standard became known as the Britannia standard. The hallmark remained in use until 1719, when King George I restored the old sterling standard for plate, although the Britannia standard was kept as an alternative.

freer, more fanciful and light. One of the dominant themes was certainly that of the shell, which was presented in different and recurring versions with edged borders and was often accompanied by foliate interwoven scrolls. Many other themes appeared, always infused with an elegant lightness: flame motifs, deeply scalloped fringe-like ornaments (lambrequins), rosettes, reworked grotesques, heads inserted in fringed cartouches and

armorial bearings. Silver was often based on the designs by Jean Bérain, *"dessinateur de la Chambre du Roi,"* which enjoyed great popularity in France. Many Régence motifs were copied, more or less faithfully, in other countries, such as the Low Countries and England,

where many Huguenot goldsmiths (including Paul de Lamerie) sought refuge, bringing with them models in vogue in Paris.

Ewer made in Switzerland (Schaffhausen, c. 1720). The body bears embossed and chased decorations with gadrooning and floral motifs. A female mask is applied to the spout.

Decorative motifs still bore traces of the late baroque, but were tempered almost to the point of appearing weakened, whereas they are really indications of the movement towards innovation and transformation that permeated all of this brief but intense historical period. Symmetry was respected, the motif of the seashell was often used, and lightness came to be the norm, although motifs were still characterized by the majesty and chiaroscuro force of the late baroque. The curved line began to dominate, with twisted and double-curved lines, edges became fringed and pierced decoration became popular. Among the most widespread motifs was the palmette, which developed from its stylized and heavy original towards a softer form, with a reconsideration of the realistic appearance of the motif itself: five leaves narrowing towards the base. In its evolution, the palmette went from compactness to having fringed edges and then piercing. Its leaves increased from five to seven so the fringing and piercing contributed to the impression that the palmette was so transformed it had become almost asymmetrical. Another fundamental element in the decorative repertory is a particular type of interlac-

The new decorative motifs of the 18th century

The reciprocal exchange of decorative repertories throughout Europe during this period was intense. France sought to impose the stylistic features of its Régence style, Holland experienced the mixture of traditional models with the new French models that arrived with Daniel Marot and the German-language countries were slowly nearing a new style as the weight of traditional motifs grew increasingly powerful. Italy was most affected by French models, but sought to simplify them and make them less imposing. In Great Britain the models that arrived with the Huguenot silversmiths with their French and Dutch backgrounds appeared alongside basic, undecorated models and re-interpretations of the late baroque. In general, this was a transitional period between the stately force of the late baroque and the calligraphic asymmetry of the rococo.

Left: George I chocolate pot made in 1715 in London by Thomas Parr I in the shape of a tapering cylinder with domed cover and carved wooden handle. A coat of arms is engraved on the side.

Bottom: Sugar bowl made by Paul de Lamerie around 1720. The surface is chased with classical motifs in the George I style. The finial of the cover repeats the shape of the bowl.

ing made by using facing foliate scrolls, which is usually associated with the standard themes of the shell, palmette or the small head. Many decorative pieces have a particular kind of background decoration: areas divided into grids of small diamond shapes at the center of which is a tiny flower or circular button.

French silver in the early 18th century

The first thirty years of the 18th century saw an increase in the production of silver in France. This phenomenon is partly explained by the desire to recover the silver that had been lost as a result of royal decrees, which brought about the almost complete destruction of wrought plate. But there is another reason: it is also significant that at this time other precious objects, such as decorated majolica and the first Western porcelains, were competing in the arena of artistic production as objects intended to adorn the homes of the wealthy. Three types of silver were made in the greatest numbers: table wares, toilet services and lighting. Table wares, numerous and sumptuous, were made according to a hierarchy based on the

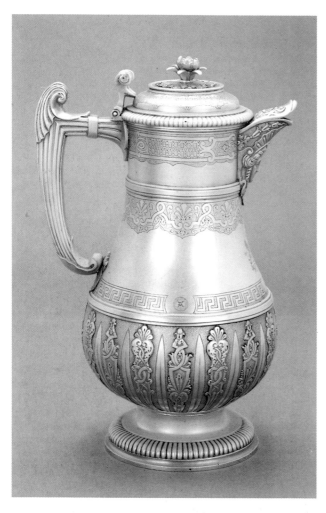

designed to hold the knife, spoon, bread, salt and so on, and the navicellas, pieces that had been popular since the medieval period, which were shaped like small ships and served to hold the king's napkin. Much care was given to the production of plates and salvers, and French silversmiths applied great variety and imagination to the detailed decoration of borders, which were chased with stylish motifs. Tureens with covers were gaining in popularity, often furnished with trays. The covers were singled out for intense and dynamic sculptural decoration. The ewer and basin, still traditional, and virtually obligatory, components of a table service were made in versions in which the ewer took the helmet shape that dates from the early 17th century. The handles, however, were made in imaginative forms of great sculptural impact. Goblets were almost always in the form of a tulip-

materials of which they were made: gold, practically reserved for the royal family, gilt silver, silver and silver plate. In practice, the quality and number of pieces increased or decreased in accordance with the buyer's social level or financial resources. Made only for the use of royalty were the *cadenas*, a sort of uncovered dish

Cup and cover made in 1724 by Paul de Lamerie. The vase-shaped body, embossed and chased with plant motifs and asymmetrical cartouches, stands on a moulded base.

shaped chalice, those made for travelling services had covers, and some had flared bases, decorated in the case of the most expensive pieces. Cruet stands made to hold crystal bottles for oil and vinegar were usually shaped like footed plates. Serving dishes, covered pans with two side handles, were widespread and often rested on a plate. Such objects enabled the silversmith to vary the decoration of the finial located at the top of the cover or to repeat the decorative motif adopted in the two handles. Thus cover and handles are decorated, but the rest of the body is elegantly smooth. A typically French silver object is the high-stemmed cup used holding boiled eggs, known as a

coquetier. These were shaped like small chalices and were almost always entirely decorated. The first double-lipped sauceboats with side handles began to appear on the table during this period, but this form was later abandoned in favour of that with a single lip and handle located at the back. Wine coolers used to chill bottles of wine were common in the homes of the well to do.

The sector of toilet plate involved a broad range of articles, from the most luxurious to the simplest, which were made throughout the century in an infinite variety designed to suit the needs and means of all buyers. Such services were originally composed of several pieces: mirror, comb

Paul de Lamerie

Paul de Lamerie (1688-1751) was born in a small town in the Low Countries, where his father, a French Huguenot, had fled to avoid persecution. A few years later the family moved to London, where in 1703 Paul began work as an apprentice in the workshop of the silversmith Pierre Platel, himself a French refugee. The first works made completely by de Lamerie bear the London hallmark and date to 1711-12; a few years later he began obtaining commissions for very lavish and important pieces from the English aristocracy. His fame grew to such an extent that the volume of business he generated hardly left him enough time to work on each piece in person, with the result that in his final years he restricted himself to producing design sketches that were then executed in his workshops. De Lamerie's finest works are those created entirely by his own hand between 1730 and 1740. The importance of his work lays in the way it introduced a breath of fresh air into the unchanging tradition of English style, creating a sort of fusion between English taste and the French grand siécle, Régence, and Louis XIV styles. De Lamerie is regarded as the foremost English interpreter of the rococo style, which he succeeded in adapting to the shapes and types of the English tradition and of which he was a master.

until 1729-30   *after 1729-30*

Sugar castor by Paul de Lamerie marked 1723 (Britannia standard) with moulded girdle and flared moulded pedestal foot; a coat of arms is engraved at the center of the body.

and cosmetic boxes of various sizes, small cups and bowls, soap dishes, perfume bottles, scissors, even a pair of candlesticks. Few complete services from the period have survived. Most of the silver made for lighting involved pairs of candlesticks, and the style of these passed from the baluster-type models based on architectural decoration, which had heavy feet and little decoration, to versions with long stems with inserted heads or masks accompanied by scrolling ribbons, a style that can be considered typically Régence.

Continental influences on English silver

It can be argued that the originality and vitality of English silver is partly the result of contributions from sources outside the

traditional English canon. Silver styles evolved slowly in England, where smiths and designers felt no need

to experiment with new models and new ideas. The stylistic uniformity of the silver made in England was reinforced by the habit of using "pattern books," collections of engraved designs intended for use in the workshop, and basing models on the Dutch baroque. The silversmiths made constant reference to these models and considered them an inexhaustible source of ideas. Around 1710 a wave of models of French derivation was introduced to England by the Huguenots, who over the course of the preceding three decades had opposed the influence of the very Dutch baroque that had formed the style of English silver over the course of the last quarter of the 17th century. Huguenot silversmiths in London formed a closed group and demonstrated great solidarity, but

SUGAR CASTORS

Castors were used to hold and "cast" not just sugar but also salt, pepper and sometimes ginger or mustard, so they were often made in three-piece sets. The earliest examples date from the second half of the 17th century, and castors as a silver type were especially popular in Great Britain, France and Russia until their popularity declined around the end of the 18th century. The earliest examples had smooth cylindrical bodies and occasional moulding; the covers were pierced in simple motifs and were held in the body by means of a sleeve inserted down to the girdle. The outline of later pieces moved increasingly towards the pearshape, with some octagonal or spiralling examples. The piercing of the covers became increasingly elegant and elaborate, and they were inserted by pressure into the bodies and held by grooves.

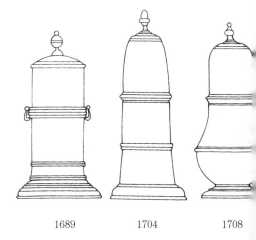

1689   1704   1708

they had to adapt their styles to meet the demands of English patrons. The Huguenot style is characterized by a perfect assimilation of the proportions so dear to classical antiquity, especially in terms of an architectural arrangement of decoration based on classical canons. It was expressed in two types: one which employed a hexagonal or octagonal section and was based on the sharp surfaces that composed the

form; the other used the same forms but was enriched, one could say covered, with numerous chased or engraved decorations as well as sculptural castings and cut-card decoration. Huguenot silversmiths made both types, basing the type chosen only on the financial means of the buyer. Their influence was of great importance to the development of English silver, but even more important and telling was the

work of the most celebrated and prolific artist of the period: Paul de Lamerie. His activity, which was concentrated in the period 1712-51, led to the total renovation of English taste. In the initial period, from 1712 to 1730, Paul de Lamerie made models with baluster forms of clear architectural derivation using a swollen bean motif in sharp relief that emphasizes and exalts the curved forms. His interest in "modern" decoration is demonstrated by a celebrated squared tray, now in London's Victoria and Albert Museum, with chased borders of extreme lightness and grace. He chose William Hogarth (1697-1764) to do the extraordinary central engraving, evidently intuiting the artist's brilliant future. Having refined the stylistic elements of the Régence style, Paul de Lamerie interpreted in a

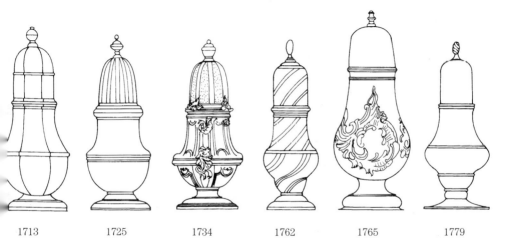

| 1713 | 1725 | 1734 | 1762 | 1765 | 1779 |

thoroughly personal way the next artistic period, the rococo, thus making a determinant contribution to the stylistic originality of English silver.

Early 18th-century Italian silver

Although limited by an attachment to late baroque models, French influences and notions and conditioning from the art of sculpture, early 18th-century Italian silver presents several original aspects.

In Naples a decree by the Viceroy Count S. Esteban, issued on August 19, 1690, and in force until 1808, regulated the use of silver. The fineness was set at about 834 thousandths, and three hallmarks were

established: one for the silversmith, one for the "consul," which guaranteed quality, and one for the guild, which guaranteed the quality of the work. This last hallmark consisted of the letters NAP surmounted by a crown with three numbers that indicated the date of manufacture (without the thousand). Even so, few pieces of silver were hallmarked during the 18th century, for the relationship of trust between buyer and smith was always close, and no one saw the need to apply marks, which also involved registration and the payment of applicable taxes. From the formal point of view, the fanciful exuberance of Neapolitan silver can be seen as a result of influence from the enormous quantity of religious silver then being made, some of it commissioned to give sumptuous adornment to churches and some of it made for private buyers. Following the recurrent epidemics much domestic plate was melted down to make silver statues and reliquaries that were donated to the church as expressions of thanks for having been spared. The outstanding object in the Neapolitan area was the impressive ornamental stand or table triumph. These fantastic compositions, with decorations clearly based on sculptural

forms, usually involved several levels of small basins, most often in the shape of seashells, used to hold spices, sweets and fruit. The entire piece, of a monumental pyramidal form, would be placed in the middle of a table and was studded with small sculptures of naiads, dolphins, tritons, sea horses and—as the crowning element, usually placed at the top to complete the imposing ornament—a character on horseback or the sea god Neptune. Even in Rome, the great weight of the tradition of late baroque sculpture was felt in the silver made during the first thirty years of the decade. This was partly a result of the fact that many silversmiths performed work for the many churches that were then being completed or had only recently been completed. The decorative breadth of Roman style is not a result only of the

The theme of the shell

The scallop shell is among the oldest and most widespread of all decorative motifs. Real shells were used a great deal in classical antiquity, especially in Roman architecture, as a covering material and for the decoration of porticoes, grottoes and architectural elements in gardens. The movement from the use of real shells to sculpted shell shapes took place at the same time. The motif was used in the Renaissance period, most of all in the architectural decorations of Brunelleschi and in pictorial works, such as the celebrated painting by Piero della Francesca in the Brera (Milan). As early as the 17th century the scallop shell was often used in decorative art and can be consid-ered one of the leading ornamental motifs of both the baroque style and the later rococo. Shells of the baroque period are compact with sharp edges, but in the first years of the 18th century the edges become fringed, and shells tend to resemble more concave leaves, and not real shells. At the end of the 18th century the shell resumed its essential form, but simplified, almost geometric, in clear accord with the rarefied neoclassical style. The shell has often been used as a container—holy water stoups in churches, salts, dessert bowls and other types of domestic plate. The shell motif's popularity was also based in part on its religious symbolism; shells were badges of pilgrimages.

magnificence of religious silver, however, and can also be traced to the work of the great artist Giovanni Giardini (1646-1721). A silversmith, he also produced important works in bronze, marble and copper. Together with Maximilian Limpach of Prague he published a large book of models of decorations for silver and bronze, the *Prontuarium Artis Argentariae*, which was used as a reference work by Roman silversmiths until the middle of the 18th century.

Flatware in the early 18th century

The shape and form of flatware continued to evolve during the first quarter of the 18th century, reflecting ongoing changes in dining habits. The process varied from one European country to another, particularly in terms of the use of the fork. Even at sumptuous court banquets little if any use was made of the fork in many areas; King Louis XIV of France ate with his fingers. Even so, the types of flatware were being diversified and were made with combinations of different materials. Flatware had been decorated primarily with motifs engraved on the surface during the 17th century, but as early as the first years of the 18th century this technique was often abandoned in favour of relief decoration, cast or chased. Engraving was used only in rare instances, most of all to mark flatware with

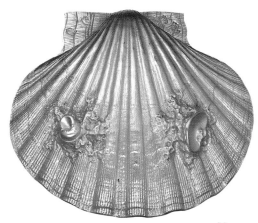

EARLY 18TH CENTURY

original brilliance. They also made for an easier connection between knife blade and handle. The pointed blades of knives were completely abandoned during this period; in France, a royal edict was passed prohibiting their production. Such rules were designed to bring an end to certain unbecoming table manners, such as using knives to clean teeth, and most of all to avoid possible threats to the safety of the host or other guests. Such armed assaults along with poisonings had long been common in the world of courts. Knives were almost invariably given the curved handles known in Great Britain as pistol handles; the name, of course, comes from the similarity of the handle to the grips of contemporary pistols. This same shape was used throughout Europe and given differing names—in Italy, for example, it was known as the "Venetian style" or "St. Mark's" handle. Some knives were made with straight handles, particularly in France, and these were decorated, usually with shells; at the very end of the handle was a button-like shape that was in reality the hammering of the tang of the blade, which extends the full length of the handle. Spoons and forks were still made in the models established at the end of the preceding centu-

coats of arms and initials. Such elements usually appear upside down on spoons and forks, since a place setting then called for the knife to be laid horizontally in front of the diner with the other pieces at the sides of the plate, but with the spoon's bowl and fork's prongs facing the

edge of the table, exactly the opposite of today's arrangement. A characteristic of flatware from the early years of the century is the frequent combination of silver with variously decorated porcelain handles; aside from not conducting heat, such handles could be washed without losing their

Piercing

The technique of piercing involves designing a decorative motif on a silver plate and then using special saws to cut away the background areas so as to obtain open spaces. There are two types of piercing: à jour and covered. A jour piercing is completely open and visually gives the same effect as lace. The operation presents difficulties in the borders, which should not be sharp. They are therefore covered with a roundish edging obtained by working directly with a chisel on the border of the plate or by carefully filing. The technique of covered piercing consists in the same operations as for à jour piercing but then placing the pierced decoration over a surface of smooth silver, which gives the effect of decorated lace that stands out against a smooth background.

ry, including trifids (with spoons that bear the classic rat tails to reinforce the joint between handle and bowl) and the uni-plat, smooth models without decoration and with handles that widen out towards a rounded end. Of English origin, these enjoyed great popularity across the Channel. The type eventually came to have a thin band running along the entire edge of the handle, in which case it is called a fil-

let. "Violin" handles, so-called from the similarity to their shape to that of the musical instrument, began in France and spread throughout Europe. These were often decorated with shells (the most common decorative motif on flatware during the early 18th century) and were thus referred to as *violon-coquille*; this shape was repeated and reworked in later years. The bowl of spoons took on a generally narrower and more tapered shape, but forks were still made with three prongs, although those with four were becoming more numerous.

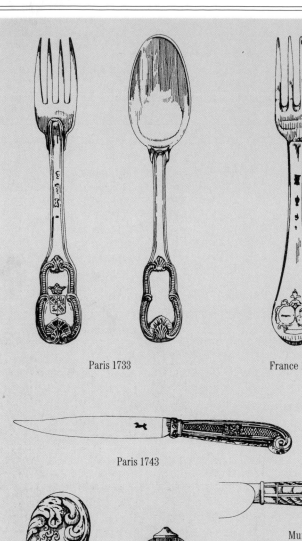

Paris 1733   France 1703   France 1710

Paris 1743

Munich 1700

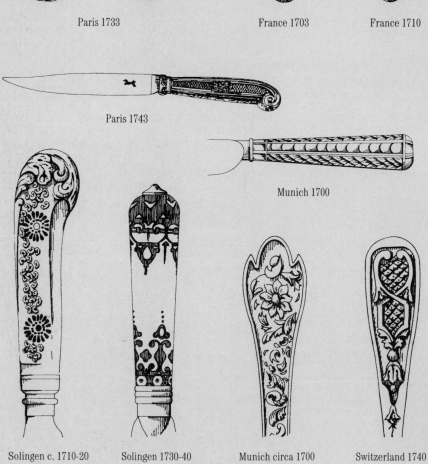

Solingen c. 1710-20   Solingen 1730-40   Munich circa 1700   Switzerland 1740

Tureen with a smooth, vaguely pear-shaped body divided in convex panels and resting on a circular, stepped base. Breslau, 1746-58.

Coffee, tea, chocolate

The custom of drinking coffee, tea and chocolate increased during the 1700s and came to involve a larger portion of society. The first of these drinks to come into use in Europe was coffee, which originated in the cultivated areas of Ethiopia and spread to the Arab lands, where drinks made from roasted coffee beans were being drunk as early as the late 14th century. Introduced to Europe by Venetian traders at the beginning of the 16th century, coffee was immediately popular. Tea, which comes from the Far East, first became popular in those countries involved in the Oriental trade: the Low Countries, England, France and Portugal. Chocolate, made of a base of cacao with sugar and milk, became known to Europe around 1528, when the conquistador Cortés brought cacao seeds home from Mexico. The ancient Aztecs made a drink from cacao seeds that they called *chocochlt*, meaning "drink of the gods." The custom of drinking these beverages saw not only the rise of special establishments for their consumption—including the coffeehouses of England and the cafés of Venice—but also the manufacture of objects to hold and serve

ASYMMETRY AND DISTORTION

These line drawings present the principal, distinctive characteristics of the rococo decorative repertory, based on asymmetry, movement, distortion and naturalism. Many of the themes were common to other periods, but they were reinterpreted in totally new ways: the line became graceful and irregular, and borders were fringed in fanciful and only slightly repeating ways.

Left: Coffeepot made in the Veneto at the height of the 18th century with a pear-shaped body, stepped base and carved wooden handle.

Bottom: Coffeepot by Paul de Lamerie, London, 1742. A classic example of the felicitous marriage of a traditional English form with rococo decorative motifs.

silver objects became itself important, as this outline was usually characterized by intense fluidity. The forms have a peculiar softening that is caused by the indefiniteness of their outlines. This trait is displayed in motifs based on torn leaves, wide folds, distorted shells and scrolls, moss and sea foam; the name of this new style, rococo, is said to come from the French *rocaille*, meaning "rock work," a reference to the rocks and other inorganic forms used in the decoration. Also of great interest are flowers, which usually tend towards stylization without, however, losing their botanic characteristics. They appear arranged as garlands, in bouquets, or individually, often with a branch and a few leaves. The three fundamental characteristics of the new style—movement, asymmetry and naturalism—are in some senses related to changes in the society of this period. Everywhere a new balance was being established within European society, in large part based on the growth of the new middle class, who were the true leaders of the economic rebirth that was underway.

them, including a wide range of silver tea, coffee and chocolate pots which were in constant competition with majolica and porcelain examples.

The new international style: rococo

The first years of the 1730s saw a complete change in European style. The style of the preceding years, with its austere lines and ever-symmetrical forms, receded, to be replaced by a style in which asymmetry dominated and in which creative fantasy based on the re-working of forms taken from the plant world became the primary basis of both shapes and decoration. Curved and sinuous lines became prevalent, so much so that the outline of

*Below: Chocolate pot,
Paris, 1747-48. The
smooth, pear-shaped
body stands on three
upright feet. The spout
is decorated with plant
motifs.*

*Below: Coffeepot by
Niels Jensen Brandt,
Fredrikstad, mid 18th
century. The pear-
shaped body is divided
in concave panels, some
of which are chased
with rococo motifs.*

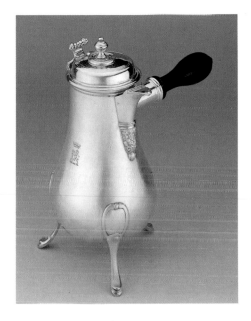

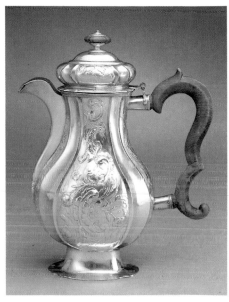

Rococo can also be seen, however, as the style of the aristocracy and the upper middle class. In truth, such grand residences as palaces and castles were no longer being built; instead, following the French example, *hôtels* and *petites maisons* were in fashion. The great halls of the past were being replaced by smaller rooms, more inviting and better suited to the needs of an increasingly polycentric social and cultural life.

The birth of the drawing room can be dated to the first half of the 17th century, but it was only at the height of the 18th century that these rooms reached their golden age. Elegant silver pieces were made to adorn these new areas, as well as dining rooms and

TYPES OF FEET

The number of feet used to support the body of an object varies, but three were usually used on small, circular objects (such as coffeepots, teapots, chocolate pots, tankards, cups and small tureens), and four, arranged symmetrically following the object's two main axes, were used on rectangular, square, oval, or large-size objects, such as tureens, cruet stands, inkstands, etc. The

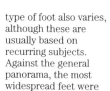

type of foot also varies, although these are usually based on recurring subjects. Against the general panorama, the most widespread feet were those shaped like animal paws, and particularly frequent are those with lion feet, hooves, and claw-and-ball feet, those with a claw grasping a sphere. Equally common are motifs of curls, spheres and, most of all in the 18th century, those of foliate scrolls.

parlours. With its refined hedonism, its intellectualism, its passion for the singular and the eccentric, the rococo style reveals the emergence of a new, large group of buyers: a public of collectors and connoisseurs who contributed to the exceptional development during this period of the applied arts, among which silver stands in the forefront.

Teapots, coffeepots, chocolate pots and others

Silver objects made for exotic drinks ranked among the most widespread types of silver during this period, and they have remained such. It is important to note the extraordinary similarity in shape between objects made in majolica and porcelain and those made

to serve the same purpose in silver. The formal relationship between objects made of the two principal materials, silver and ceramic, is close, since the shapes are almost identical, although the material appearance is unequivocally quite different. Coffeepots were first made in an elongated tapering cylinder with a spout departing the body about

---

**THE EVOLUTION
IN SHAPE OF
THE ENGLISH
COFFEEPOT IN
THE 18TH CENTURY**
The coffeepot is among the silver types that have enjoyed the most fortune in time and different geographic regions, assuming particular characteristics and evolving into original, successful shapes. A good sense of the coffeepot's evolution is offered by the different shapes taken by the English

coffeepot in the course of the 18th century. The coffeepots from the first years of the century are tapering cylinders with smooth, undecorated sides. The cover, hinged to the body, is domed or slightly flaring. Beginning in the 1720s, the coffeepot was often made in octagonal section, the neck of the spout became more elaborate, spouts were shaped, and the finial of the cover became

larger and worked. In the second half of the 1730s models appeared with a stepped base; the

form evolved further, and around the middle of the century pear-shaped bodies appeared. The deco-

Below: Pair of sorbet cups with spoons, Naples, 1753-54. The flaring of the cups becomes more accentuated at the top.

Below: Toilet box by Antoine-Sébastien Durand, Paris, 1747. The richly decorated rounded body with cover stands on a stepped base.

halfway up and with a conical, or domed, cover hinged at the handle. An English example that dates from 1681-82 is of great simplicity and bears no decoration except for an engraved dedicatory inscription. At the beginning of the 18th century decoration began to appear around the spout and in the areas where the handle was joined to the body. Around 1720 the shape began moving from the tapering cylinder to a more octagonal form.

During the rococo period, although the coffeepot kept its elongated shape and its spout at the middle of the body, it began to fill with decorations, most of all on the lower part of the body, where the decorations could make use of the slope, and at the spout, which became almost entirely covered with decoration. The base remained generally circular, and over the course of time it grew larger and took on a flared form, contributing increased lightness to the whole. Such models are typically English. In France, coffeepots tended to be pear shaped, standing on three feet with side-mounted straight handles, and the spout was located above,

ration became more marked, sometimes covering not just the borders and areas of handle and spout fittings, but the entire surface. The rigour of the neoclassical style preferred sober, linear forms; popular were urn-shaped bodies and the *cul de poule*, standing on reversed-funnel bases. The handles, more or less elaborate, were usually of ebony or carved wood, for obvious reasons of heat insulation.

ENGLISH 18TH-CENTURY HALLMARKS

The table on the opposite page lists the types of hallmarks used on English silver in the 18th century. By law, each piece of silver had to bear four hallmarks, indicating the city of origin, standard of the metal, year of fabrication, and silversmith who made the work. In the first column at left are the city hallmarks. In the 18th century England was divided into ten principal guilds with twenty-odd secondary guilds; each city had its own hallmark, which over time underwent only slight variations in detail, except for the period from 1697 to 1720, when these marks were replaced by the Britannia standard mark. In the second column are the assay marks, represented since 1544 by the lion passant; once again an exception is made for the period from 1697 to 1720, when the standard of plate was raised from 92.5 to 95.8 percent, and the lion passant was replaced by a hallmark known as the lion's head erased (a lion's head in profile).

The cities of Edinburgh and Glasgow present exceptions to these rules.

Until 1758 in Edinburgh (1) the assay hallmark used was the initials of the assay warden; from 1759 to today this has been replaced by a mark showing a thistle within a shield. Glasgow (2) did not have a separate assay office until 1819; until then, the assay mark was included with the date letter, shaped like an S for sterling or standard and then an O.

In 1784 a new tax was put on silver, and a fifth mark was added to signify the duty had been paid. This mark showed the king's head in profile; the first example was George III. The other columns give the date letter marks, represented each year by a different letter of the alphabet. When the alphabet is complete the series begins again from the beginning (from A), changing the "type" of the letter and the

From 1697 to 1720 the city hallmarks were replaced by Britannia, and the assay marks were replaced by the lion's head erased.

shape of the shield. For reasons of space the complete alphabets are not reproduced; instead a letter representative of the series is given, with indication of the date the series began and ended. For example, in London the F written in a shield is part of an alphabet in use from 1715 (with the letter A) until 1735 (with the letter V); beginning in 1736 the shape of the shield changed, as did the form of the letters. Some alphabets were not completed, such as some used in York and Sheffield. In Glasgow, where the date letter was mixed with the assay mark, the alphabet is composed of a series of variations on the letters S and O.

On page 160 is a table of 19th-century English hallmarks based on the same arrangement.

Below are reproductions of several maker's marks used by silversmiths active in London in the 18th century; these are composed of the silversmith's initials and a personal emblem. The date given beneath the hallmark and name is when the hallmark was registered.

Lawrence Jones
1697

Thomas Sadler
1701

Richard Greene
1703

Simon Patin I
1717

Thomas Morse
1718

William Darker
1731

Nicholas Sprimont
1743

Edward Wakelin
1747

Robert & William Peaston
1756

John Gorham
1757

CITY	STANDARD	ANNUAL LETTERS			
LONDON		from A 1716 to V 1735	from A 1736 to U 1755	from A 1756 to U 1775	from A 1776 to U 1795
YORK		from A 1700 (incom.)	from A 1700 (incom.)	from A 1776 to L 1786	from A 1776 to L 1786
EXETER		from A 1701 to Z 1724	from A 1725 to Z 1748	from A 1749 to Z 1772	from A 1773 to Y 1796
NEWCASTLE		from A 1721 to T 1739	from A 1721 to T 1739	from A 1759 to Z 1790	from A 1759 to Z 1790
CHESTER		from A 1701 to Z 1725	from A 1726 to Z 1750	from A 1751 to Y 1775	from A 1776 to V 1796
BIRMINGHAM		from A 1773 to Z 1797	from A 1773 to Z 1797	from A 1773 to Z 1797	from A 1798 to Z 1823
SHEFFIELD		from E 1773 to V 1798	from E 1773 to V 1798	1788 (incom.)	1794 (incom.)
EDINBURGH	(1)	from A 1705 to Z 1729	from A 1730 to Z 1754	from A 1755 to Z 1778	1779
GLASGOW	(2)	1723	1743	1756	1776
DUBLIN		from A 1720 to Z 1746	from A 1720 to Z 1746	from A 1747 to Z 1772	from A 1773 to Z 1796

ROCOCO

One of a pair of three-branched candelabra of intense rococo sculptural value by the silversmith Charles Frederick Kandler, London, 1738.

immediately beneath the base of the cover and projecting only slightly from the body. The Venetian coffeepot can be taken as typical of Italian production, with its baluster form and body with vertical ribbing, its spout located above and slightly projecting, and with its slightly flared octagonal base. In the later rococo style the body of coffeepots tended to have twisted ribbing, and flat bases were replaced by three feet.

The teapot underwent a remarkable development in England during this period, as a result of the widespread consumption of tea in coffeehouses, which were becoming increasingly popular: there were nearly two thousand in London in the early years of the 18th century. Some sources date the custom of drinking tea to 1708 and Tom's Coffee House in Devereux Court, owned by Thomas Twining. This shop, a popular meeting place of eminent lawyers and their clients, enjoyed enormous success, and tea started to become England's favourite beverage.

The form of the teapot, with the so-called bullet, or compressed spherical, shape, the long spout leaving from the bottom of the body, rear handle and cover, is tied to Chinese ceramic teapots. The earliest known English teapot is dated 1670 and is, in reali-

ty, a coffeepot of the tapering-cylinder type; however, it bears an engraved inscription that calls it "a silver teapot." The early 18th century saw the use of the baluster form, also called the pear shape, which was very functional because the most voluminous area of the body is the lower part. The spout was still long and began from the middle of the globular body. In the rococo period the form tended to soften,

and sometimes the globular body became spherical; around the 1740s the form was reversed, with the more voluminous part above, and the base made thin and tapering. Decoration, still rather restrained, was concentrated on the upper part of the body and involved the cover and the spout attachment.

The shape of the chocolate pot, very common in Italy and France and less so in England, differs very lit-

Bottom: Candlestick from Genoa from the second half of the 18th century. The base and stem are powerfully ribbed in a sinuous movement broken by decorations of plant motifs.

Below: Bedside hand warmer in silver with a rounded body with pierced cover and horizontal turned-wood handle. Turin, 1760-70.

tle from that of the coffeepot. It tends to be a little less pot-bellied and often has a straight handle of turned wood fitted at right angles to the spout. The major difference is that the finial is often hinged or pivoted so as to open for a stirrer with which to mix the boiling milk and bits of chocolate or ground cacao. The handle of the stirrer had decoration matching that of the finial.

Candlesticks and candelabra

Candlesticks are among the silver forms that underwent the greatest development of interesting forms during this period, taking advantage of the sinuous lines of rococo

taste. The plate-like base of candlesticks was elaborated into sculptural forms exhibiting notable movement, often twisting, along with a certain tendency to swollen forms. This characteristic is often found in examples from the Veneto area of Italy, whereas in England the base plate is often simple. Much attention was given to the shaft, or stem, which maintained its columnar form but with an added central swelling. Later the stem was given a twisted movement using continuously spiralling and curved lines that spread upwards from a bell-shaped base and travel along the stem to end at the mouth without a form to end their continuity.

This bizarre and imaginative form was the favourite for the candlesticks produced in great numbers by Dutch silversmiths. The fluidity and continuity of rococo lines joined to deco-

rative elements with fluid movements is often found in two-branched candlesticks and candelabra with three or more branches. It is clear that the presence of arms to hold the candles was eminently suitable to plastic treatment as curving branches, with the curved lines emphasized by leafy elements. The mouth that holds the candle at the end of the stem is often given the appearance of a floral bud or corolla. The fluid and expressive lines were also applied to important variations in the stem, which from a swollen, twisted column came to assume anthropomorphic shapes, leading to the use of cast stems with caryatid figures. Stems in the form of a beautiful girl emerging from the stand within interwoven vegetation were very popular, most of all in France, and these were repeated in England, particularly as seen in

67

ROCOCO

The decorative repertory of rococo

Rejection of the straight line is the most characteristic element in the decorative repertory of the rococo, which is based instead on curved, sinuous lines formed with the heavy use of a certain typical stylistic element. This element is a kind of C, comparable to the shape of an ear, and it is employed works by the silversmiths of the Le Sage dynasty.

Another important modification of the stem consists in the insertion above the base of pleasing sculptural figures. The cupids that the great French silversmith François-Thomas Germain adopted in his works are considered to be among the outstanding examples of this style.

The addition of sculptural figures eventually led to the total transformation of the stem, which became a single form joined together with the rest of the candlestick. This search for global forms in which volume and decoration form a single whole found its highest expression in the candlesticks made to designs by the celebrated French artist Juste Aurèle Meissonnier, whose volumes of engravings were crucial in spreading the rococo style throughout Europe.

Pear-shaped pitcher with chased and embossed decoration of a landscape within a cartouche. Attributed to D.C. Fueter, New York, c. 1770.

various parts reveals that the whole is formed by the same elements, equal and repeated and variously and fantastically arranged. Themes of flowers, vine leaves and vines are often associated with foliate scrolls as well as the heavy use of curls.

Flowers are not presented frontally, in a static way, but are seen foreshortened in a dynamic way, with great attention to the details of parts. The dynamism of this decorative style is accentuated through the use of spiralling forms in twisting movements that, enlivening the surfaces, both dispel any weightiness of form and give an impression of continuous surface variation. The asymmetry, fantasy and dynamism of rococo decorative motifs contribute to giving works in silver a considerable number of

in various ways: simply, in complex forms, interwoven, elongated, stretched. Two of these Cs joined but facing in opposite directions create a kind of S that can be further complicated by another basic stylistic element: the curl. This curl is in part taken from the plant world and

in part represents a distortion of the classical scroll. At first glance, the general impression of rococo decoration is one of complexity: an interweaving of leaves, leafy scrolls, S motifs and elements taken directly from the large repertory of flowers and fruit. However, a closer examination of the

---

LOUIS XV DECORATIONS

Much of the decorative repertory of the French Louis XV style is based on the widespread works of Juste Aurèle Meissonnier (1695-1750), who created many models for goldsmiths (he was one himself) before taking on the prestigious post of "dessinateur de la Chambre du Roi." The most recurrent motifs are, on one hand, those that take inspiration from the plant

world, and on the other those typically *rocaille*: curling lines and C-shapes harmoniously combined, infinite variations on the shell theme, garlands, flowering vines, festoons, intertwined

branches, foliate scrolls, ribbons and fluting in sinuous lines. All these elements are characterized by a marked asymmetry and are combined fancifully to constitute a light and

elegant whole. Form and decoration often become one, mixed in a sort of plastic symbiosis in which they overlap and replace each other, making it difficult to tell them apart.

ROCOCO

Ewer and basin by Martin Satzger, Augsburg, around the middle of the 18th century. The rich decoration is obtained with embossing and chasing.

characteristic traits that make the style relatively easy to identify.

The fact that the decorative elements were not rigidly codified but were instead seen as offering themselves openly to the infinite possible variants inherent in their being plants, free to take varying form, led to a high level of creative freedom, which is clearly manifested in the fantastic and rarely repetitive lines of the rococo style. During its latest phase, the style became overburdened, far less restrained and willingly capricious. It should not surprise anyone that the decorative follies of the rococo led to a reaction based on neoclassical style.

Ewers and basins

The use of the ewer and basin continued during the rococo period for the traditional set still performed its double functions of utility

18TH-CENTURY HANDLES

Because silver conducts heat well, the widespread popularity of tea and coffee services during the 18th century required the use of handles in some insulating material so that the pots, with their boiling liquid contents, could be easily handled. Wood was the preferred material, for it can be easily shaped and carved in various forms; handles were also made

of ebony or ivory, but only rarely, and only for pieces of great importance. The most common were S-forms, double-C shapes, curls, with or without elbow, and swan necks; these often have small protruding tabs on which to rest the thumb during the operation of pouring. Where heat conduction was not a primary consideration, handles were still made in silver, and owing to progress made in techniques of casting, these were made in new styles of notable plastic expression.

Bottom: Ewer from Oporto, third quarter of 18th century. The helmet-shaped body is richly decorated with rocaille motifs. The handle is composed of a series of reversed scrolls.

Below: Ewer in gilt silver, S. & J. Crespell, London, 1767. The body is richly embossed with decorations of putti, flowers, fruit and masks.

and ornament. They were useful since most people still needed to rinse their fingers during a meal; ornamental because their imposing size made them well suited to the exaltation of the refined taste—and financial status—of the host. The general lines of the ewer and basin changed little and showed the weight of tradition. It is worthwhile remembering that the ewer and basin were always directly related to the over-decorated 16th-century examples from Italy, Spain and Portugal, as well as to the typical helmet-shaped models that were made in large numbers in Germany, the Netherlands and England. In examining the rococo ewer attention must also be given to its various component parts: the base, body and handle. The base is a domed foot, which in early versions was joined directly to the body. The form of the base then changed, becoming swollen and higher, and the juncture with the body was no longer direct but was obtained using a knot in the form of architectural moulding. This knot served to make the general form of

the ewer more graceful. With the further development of decorative motifs becoming increasingly animated and complex, the base became an element composed of asymmetrical curls and scrolls rising to join directly the lower part of the body of the ewer without an element to mark the juncture. In effect, the rococo decoration of the base embraces the body and concentrates the ewer's decoration on the lower area in a way that creates a kind of upward movement that accentuates the vertical thrust of the piece. The bodies of ewers were made in two fundamental styles: the helmet model, with its broad projecting spout, and the baluster model, with its swollen lower part and spout almost hidden by the

ROCOCO

rim decoration. This second type, most of all in French examples, has a hinged cover, similar to those found on tankards. The decoration of the body is based on the curving, asymmetrical lines of the lower part of the ewer and displays striking plasticity, as though it were a corolla

of support for the rest of the ewer. In many examples this decoration involves only the lower area; the rest of the body is almost smooth, and the decoration begins again on the upper border, accentuating the sense of the fringed line. Ewer handles are of two basic types. The

first is a handle with two points of attachment to the body, one in the bellied area of the lower body and the other on the upper edge. The second, quite striking, model has a single attachment on the upper border of the ewer from which the handle extends in the form of a large C that balances

FINIALS

Being small, finials often pass unobserved, but they nevertheless deserve attention. Finials fulfil a specific function: they offer something to grip in order to raise the cover, whether it is free or hinged to the body, as in the case of tea- and coffeepots. This functional value is united, especially in important pieces of display plate, with

an explicitly decorative role. Located at the center of the cover, the finial is the apex of the piece, the final rounding-off of the entire object. Obtained most often by casting using sand moulds and finished by chasing to create the smallest details, finials often present plastic forms of great impact and exquisite refinement.

use of tea in Europe had a great influence on the applied arts, especially during the 18th century and most of all with ceramics and silver. The custom of drinking tea led to the introduction of new types of silver associated with its preparation and service. These included not just teapots and kettles, but milk jugs, sugar bowls and even cups (these proved impractical due to silver's conductivity and were abandoned in favour of porcelain cups). There were also tea caddies, which evolved from simple containers for storing tea into small, finely wrought pieces belonging to table services and travel kits. The first boxes for holding tea reached England with shipments from the Far East, and they came to be called caddies because they could hold one *catty* of tea, a *catty* being an Asian unit of weight.

The most common basic form is a tall box, and in some highly refined examples the decoration is composed of a symbiosis of rococo motifs with images clearly drawn from the Oriental style. This is the case with several examples made by Paul de Lamerie in 1748 that constituted a popular and much-imitated prototype. There are also tea caddies composed of a small casket or fitted case that contains three urn-shaped boxes; two smaller ones to hold the leaves of two types of tea and a larger one to hold sugar. The shape of these sets, thanks to the particular form of the urns, was well suited to bear the typical stylistic elements of the rococo.

Hanaps

A particular kind of silver object made in Russia during this period was a kind of cup and cover known as the hanap. This cannot be taken as part of the panorama of rococo silver, for its form displays the heavy weight of tradition. In fact, it can be traced back to the many highly elaborate

the thrust of the projecting spout. The basin is always in perfect decorative harmony with the ewer, with the greatest emphasis given to the border, where decoration is concentrated that repeats the general decorative scheme of the ewer.

Tea caddies

The importation and increasingly widespread

ROCOCO

examples of covered cups produced by the German school of the 16th and 17th centuries, which were true Gothic-baroque monuments exalting the splendour and power of their owners. An outstanding example of these is the celebrated Maximilian Cup, made in Nuremberg in 1510, which stands fully 56 centimeters high. Russian models display a curious similarity to these, and their decorative repertory has no direct relation to rococo style, but their complicated forms and their bizarreness held a fascination for the Russian world. Furthermore, even if not truly rococo, Russian hanaps display the sense of fantasy and the picturesque and exuberant spirit typical of the rococo.

This type of object can be divided into two principal types: a cup shaped like a

THE EVOLUTION OF THE SHAPE OF THE ENGLISH SUGAR BOWL
Sugar bowls are among those types of English silver that have undergone the most marked evolution in shape. The simplified designs of important models presented here, dating from the end of the 17th century to the early years of the 19th, illustrate the evolution of these containers.

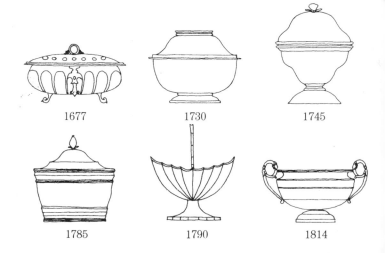

1677

1730

1745

1785

1790

1814

Left: Coffeepot with spiralling pear-shaped body standing on three scroll feet joined to the body with foliate masks. The finial is in the shape of a rose. Mons (Belgium), 1765.

Bottom: Coffeepot from Holland with pear-shaped body and spout tight to the neck with rocaille motifs. Amsterdam, 1772.

The animated rococo

With the passing of time, the rococo style went from adapting *rocaille* decorative motifs to already existing forms to changing forms through decoration. This led to the invention of new forms inspired by the complete unification of form and decoration. The question then arises of whether it was the decoration, taken as an element of fantasy, that created the new forms, taken as the practical element, or if the new forms caused an evolution of the decorative repertory. The most reasonable answer is that initially the rococo stylistic elements were applied to existing forms, and then these elements gradually expanded and finally took over the forms, achieving a complete integration with

grape cluster and a cup with combined pear-shaped elements that form two cups, a larger one and a secondary one that served as cover. Because of its two cups, this latter type is also known as a "friendship cup." The form of the bases is reminiscent of Gothic multifoil bases. The characteristic trait of these is the element used to unite the base to the body of the cup. This element is often shaped like an anthropomorphic figure, an angel or graceful putto. This element creates a sharp break between the swollen cone forming the base and the body of the cup. This dividing element is the most rococo aspect of this type, since the small figures belong to the repertory of fanciful 18th-century sculptures.

One highly individual trait of Russian silvers is the fact that covers are almost always topped by the Russian imperial eagle.

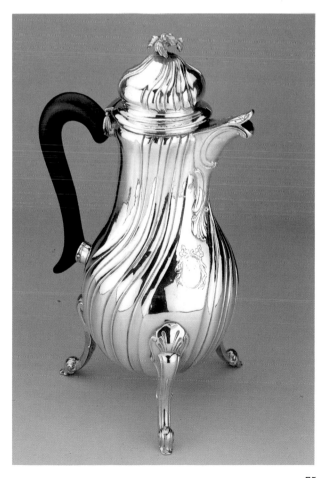

ROCOCO

Covered jewel box made in Russia, 1759-84. The oval, convex body is embossed and chased with rocaille *and plant motifs.*

York silversmith Myer Myers (1723-95) are of interest. The bodies of these are of the tapering-cylinder type dating back to the late 17th century, but he added components of pure rococo style to this body in the attachment of the spout to the body of the coffeepot as well as in the attachment of the handle, particularly the lower attachment, where the handle's projecting curl gives a sense of movement. In Flemish and Dutch examples, the sense of movement is achieved by undulating, spiral ribbing across a pear-shaped body. Analysis of this ribbing is important, since there was a movement from wide ribs to narrower, more compact ones that contributed a greater sense of movement. In Italy, this movement was further enhanced by using the typical swan-neck spout

them. The end result of this progressive movement was a complete identification between form and decoration, which became practically inseparable: the entire object was made fluid, its various parts were merged, giving the whole a sense of movement. This movement was obtained using undulating curves acquired with the widespread use of spiralling ribbing. American, Flemish, Dutch and Italian coffeepots offer good examples of this evolution—the selection is broad because a great deal of silver from this period has survived. The coffeepots made by the New

ROCOCO NATURALISM

Constant reference to nature is one of the principal aspects of the decorative repertories at the height of the 18th century. Nature served as an invaluable source of inspiration during other periods, but in the rococo period references to nature became almost constant, and freed of any ties with classical schemes they provided freer and more fanciful interpretations of the plant world.

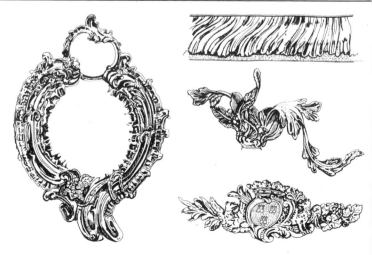

along with the undulating ribbing. The fluid contours of this spout, which extends beyond the body, are of primary importance as they both animate the piece and give it an extraordinary sense of balance.

Types of coffeepots

The production of coffeepots was intense in every area of Europe during this period, especially at the height of the 18th century. The popular models can be divided into four basic types: those with amphora-shaped bodies, also known as baluster types; those with pear-shaped bodies; those with twisted pear-shaped bodies; and finally those of smaller size. The last type differs from the other three only in terms of size; rather than the usual 30-40 centimeters of height, they are only 13-20. These small coffeepots

are sometimes referred to as *egoiste* pots, since they held enough coffee for a single person. The notion itself seems curious, since coffee was traditionally a beverage consumed in the company of friends. These rare pieces sometimes appear as part of two-piece sets along with a normal-sized coffeepot of identical form and decoration. The base of the coffeepot can be a solid plinth or three feet shaped vaguely like claws. The bodies were made in the three shapes described above. The spout can be an integral part of the body or can be a separately attached element; those attached usually extend upwards from the more rounded lower part of the body, and such long spouts are called swan- or bird-neck spouts. Covers are either hinged at the handle or completely free. Hinged covers often bear thumb-pieces, short projecting devices, a kind of tab, with which the cover could be raised using the thumb. The cover was topped by a separate element, both decorative and functional, that was sometimes small, like a little finial, and sometimes more imposing and sculptural, practically a small statue. The handle, often of wood, is attached to the body immediately under the border of the cover and at the widest area of the body. Analysis of these compo-

77

nents, their intrinsic characteristics, the lines of the handle, the application of the decoration, the quality of the sculptural parts, as well as the balance among the various parts represent the basic elements with which the quality of these silver coffeepots is judged.

Special English silver

The period from 1730 to 1770, sometimes known in England as the mid-Georgian, saw an extraordinary proliferation of special types of silver for various particular uses. Aside from their great cultural interest, these items reveal how

the love for table furnishings came to be expressed in objects with specific functions. Wine drinking and tasting, for example, involved large basins into which wine was poured so it could breathe during decanting; small tasting cups known as wine tasters; bottle tickets, or wine or spirit labels, small chained labels engraved with the names of wines and spirits that were hung around bottle necks; "bottle plates," or coasters; and finally wine funnels, which were used in decanting wines. Among other curiosities were the various containers for cream, known variously as cream jugs, cream boats, cream pails and most famous of

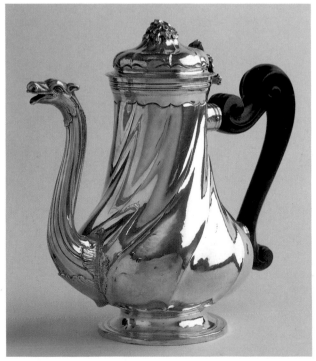

Opposite top:
Coffeepot with embossed
spiralling body and
spout tight to the neck
ending in a lion's head.
By Carlo Francesco
dell'Acqua, Milan,
1750-60.

Opposite bottom:
Coffeepot with pear-
shaped potbellied body
and elongated spout
that ends in an animal
head. Genoa, 1758.

Bottom: Cow creamer
by John Schuppe,
London, 1761. The sur-
face is opacified in imi-
tation of the hide of the
animal. On the back is a
small hinged lid.

The cow creamer

The cow creamer is a type of small cream jug modelled in the shape of a cow. Influenced by Dutch silver, these jugs were made particularly during the 1760s by the famous English silversmith John Schuppe, who worked between 1754 and 1768 in London, where he registered his hallmark in 1753 (a rectangle containing the letters I and S in cursive script). Cow creamers are filled through a small opening in the animal's back, concealed beneath a hinged lid; the cream is served by taking hold of the conveniently ring-shaped tail and pouring the contents through a hole in the animal's mouth. Although almost all of Schuppe's creamers are of the same shape, there are small variations in detail: the hinged lid on the back may be either plain or embellished with floral decoration, and a life-size figure of a fly is almost always applied to the lid's center. Numerous copies of Schuppe's jugs were made, particularly during the 19th century, but these inevitably lack the charm of the originals.

all, the cow creamer in the shape of a cow. There were also mazarines, plates that fit into a large oval dish and were pierced to strain off excess cooking liquor from fish. A particularly important group is composed of baskets, many of which were pierced and chased to look like wickerwork. With or without handles, these differ according to use, such as cake baskets and fruit baskets. The most interesting object was, perhaps, the epergne, a monumental centerpiece composed of a silver frame supporting a central basket or bowl accompanied by several branches supporting smaller baskets or bowls. These could be used to serve dessert or fruit, sweetmeats, or pickles. Salt cellars and mustard pots were also included in table services and were made in several types. In fact, the models then introduced were the originals for the forms still given table service pieces today. The strainers used for the juice of lemons or oranges are examples of how great care was bestowed on even the smallest details of the table setting.

The creators of rococo decoration

The extraordinary creative imagination demonstrated by rococo silversmiths was in part a result of pattern books, which served as a constant source of reference for designs and which, passing from workshop to workshop, came into use on such a vast scale as to make rococo a truly international style. The style is generally considered to have reached its zenith during the period 1730-45, years that coincide with the publication and diffusion of important collections of ornamental models. The copperplate engravings in these works were enormously popular. The leading creator of these

designs was Juste Aurèle Meissonnier (1675-1750), who was born in Turin but lived in Paris, where he worked as a designer for Louis XV. An inventive and multi-talented artist, he worked in painting, sculpture, architecture and goldworking. His fame is primarily a result of his goldworking and his creation of decorative motifs. He is considered one of the creators of the rococo style and is given much credit for the spread of the style throughout Europe. His important works include the *Book of Plant Motifs*, published in 1732-33, and the celebrated *Book of Ornaments*, published in 1734. His influence in the field of silver was enormous and basic, for his designs were revolutionary, irrever-

ent and playful. Although Meissonnier is considered the leading promulgator of rococo design, he was by no means the only one. Less well known but not necessarily less important were Jacques de Lajoue and Pierre-Edme Babel. Born in Paris, Lajoue (1687-1761) was a painter of architecture and landscapes, a decorator, and a unique character. A man of great originality, he was among the leaders of the rebellion against the heaviness of forms and conventional and codified austerity of the Louis XIV style. Although

on close terms with Meissonnier and the artists Watteau and Gillot, he worked mostly alone, and his influence on the rococo style is due to a splendid album of decorative models, the *Book of Scrolls*, which was published in 1734. Pierre-Edme Babel (c. 1720-75), also Parisian, was a figure of central importance to decoration. A designer of decorations, a goldsmith and an engraver of etchings, he concentrated all his activity on the design and elaboration of rococo stylistic elements. His masterfully engraved

Opposite bottom: Belgian chocolate pot from the third quarter of the 18th century. It stands on three curling foliate feet and has a fruit-shaped finial.

Bottom left: Chocolate pot, Lille, 1757. The pear-shaped body is animated by smooth, rounded sections; the same movement is repeated in the stepped cover with its finial of a foliate fruit.

Bottom right: Chocolate pot from Turin, third quarter of the 18th century. The body with sinuous lines stands on three feet with scrolled foliate masks. The spout is tight to the body with rocaille motifs.

works show signs of Italian influence. The title of his *Capricci pittoreschi* (Picturesque Caprices), published in 1734, recalls the traditional themes of Venetian paintings. This overview of designers of decorative motifs must also include a book that may have been less noble than its predecessors but that had the fortune of being readily accepted by silversmiths, for the decorative examples it presented were more restrained and thus easier to make. This was the *Book of Rocaille Forms and Cartouches*, designed by Jean Mondon and published in 1736. In England, the circulation of preparatory designs and drawings by Paul de Lamerie, as well as his works themselves— all characterized by a pro-

fusion of exuberant and sometimes bizarre motifs— constituted a "book" of ideal models to which the many imitators of this master made frequent reference. The English rococo cannot be considered without mention of his crucial influence.

Mirrors and inkstands

Objects in silver made specifically for the use of women are principally toilet articles; those made for men are usually desk accessories. The mirror included as part of the traditional toilet service offered a perfect form for the expression of rococo's almost breezy dexterity. First of all, the shape of the mirror provided a suitable form for a fluid series of light cartouches.

Decoration was located at the top of the mirror, in the area below, and in the small feet on which it stood. The decoration of the top is almost always of great plastic value, obtained using the concept of superimposition. Along the upper border might be decorations based on motifs taken from the plant world, such as roses or foliate scrolls, and over these would be a sculptural form of pleasing volume. Among the favoured themes of these sculptures are those—typical of items made ladies during this period—that make symbolic reference to love. A little after 1760, preference came to be given the bows and quivers with arrows that are the weapons of Cupid, god of love, and kissing doves. These symbols enjoyed such

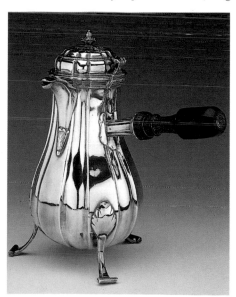

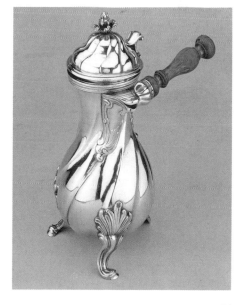

ROCOCO

decoration was thus applied most of all to the stand, the borders and feet of which become the principal elements as they were suitable to the application of the typical decoration of flowers, vines and fringed shells. The small bell sometimes included in these desk sets proved adaptable to the spiraling movement

Antoine-Sébastian Durand

Antoine-Sébastian Durand, without doubt one of the leading French silversmiths of the 18th century, became a master in 1740 and was active in the craft until 1785. He made many pieces of display plate, often on commissions from members of the aristocracy of various countries, in particular the king of Portugal, and is considered by many to be one of the most important interpreters of the rococo style. Standing out among his many known works is a pair mustard pots shaped like cupids pushing carts, made in 1750 for Madame de Pompadour and today preserved in the Gulbenkian Foundation of Lisbon. Lisbon's National Museum of Antique Art preserves a ewer and basin in gilt silver from 1752-53, often considered an outstanding example of Durand's skill because of its fanciful decoration with rococo motifs. In 1764 Durand made the first sword for the young duke of Berry, future king of France as Louis XVI.

enormous popularity that they can be found even on pieces made late in the 19th century. The decoration of the lower part of the mirror frame is almost always restrained, for most attention was given the imposing decoration of the upper border. The feet were well suited to the application of rococo stylistic elements. These are often made using highly foliate reversed scrolls bearing flowers that, in the most prestigious examples, are joined to the frame with knotted bows.

Desk inkstands did not prove as readily adaptable to the usual flowing stylistic elements of the rococo. The primary difficulty is that inkstands are made to serve a very precise function and require containers of a definite shape. The

Below: Cup by Jean-Baptiste-François Chéret, Paris, 1767-77. The spherical cup stands on a cylindrical stem on a pedestal foot, all richly decorated with embossing and chasing.

Bottom: Inkstand by Eliza Godfrey, London, 1756. The tray bears two glass containers mounted in silver and a bell with a baluster handle.

Inkstands

Although several examples of silver inkstands are known that date from the second half of the 17th century, inkstands became truly popular and widespread during the 18th century. In 18th-century Europe, the ability to write letters or compose epigrams became a source of pride for members of both the aristocracy and the upper middle classes, and inkstands thus became one of the most important items of decoration in the elegant homes of the period. Made of various materials (marquetry, bronze, porcelain, silver, or gold) in a variety of different shapes, they are often the work of famous artists. They usually include a set of containers that made to hold ink, the sand used to dry it, the seals for sealing letters, and the quill pens used in writing. Some examples include a candle- or taperstick and a small bell with which to summon the servant responsible for delivering correspondence. The earliest silver inkstands are fairly similar in shape and are of simple construction: a small, usually rectangular tray standing on small feet placed at each of the four corners on which the different containers stand or to which they were attached. As demand grew, the inkstand diversified into different and increasingly sophisticated forms, ranging from the casket type, in which the containers are protected by a hinged lid, to the type equipped with a pierced-silver compartment in which the glass containers are housed. Other types appeared towards the end of the century, the most original of which was perhaps the so-called globe inkstand, composed of a sphere resting on a pedestal the upper section of which rotates on a pivot to reveal the writing accessories within.

of the rococo; in particular the cone of the bell presented a surface well suited to spiralling ribbing.

Table silver: the serving dish

The problem of keeping food warm in an attractive table piece was solved using a squat, round or oval bowl with a cover and two side handles. This particular type of table dish was used both at table and for meals eaten while travelling. Such pieces are composed of a body, usually very simple in terms of decoration, with two handles on opposite sides; a cover, where most of the decoration is concentrated; and finally a finial atop the cover, this too of great decorative interest. The rococo style produced charming examples that can be judged by their decorative repertory. In France, the serving dishes made by the celebrated silversmith Thomas Germain are justifiably famous. These have simple, basic lines, with handles in the shape of coiling snakes, with the same snake motif forming a ring over the cover. On other examples made in France, the handles are decorated instead with the owner's family coat of arms. In Italy, these handles were usually shaped like seashells or elongated plant elements, sometimes pierced to increase the grace and lightness of the piece. In Russia, this type takes a more solid form, and the decoration is applied to the body of the bowl as well as to the cover. The element of greatest formal interest was the decoration of the cover. Italian examples in particular display the typically rococo longing for a sense of movement. The cover assumes a dome shape, is broad and well delineated and is not flattened. To obtain the effect of movement, the decoration is often based on rays of gadrooning or on a decorative strip along the lower edge of the cover decorated with fluidly curving elements. In some cases the cover is divided into eight segments, always using curved and twisting lines, entirely decorated with flowering vines and fringed cartouches.

The sculptural figures that stand atop the covers of these pieces give abundant proof of creative imagination joined to the quest for realistic expressions taken from the plant or animal world. Thus we find artichokes, roses, flower panicles, interwoven leaves animated by a vertical thrust, as well as animals and birds. The success of these pieces can be judged by how well this decoration relates to the

Opposite top: Serving dish made in Moscow, 1757. The circular body bears two pierced wing-handles; both body and cover are densely decorated with rocaille motifs.

Opposite bottom: Serving dish by Michele Antonio Merlo, Turin, 1768-78. The smooth circular body has two handles in the form of foliate scrolls; the cover bears a rose finial with leaves.

Below: Serving dish with circular body with sinuous ribbing interrupted by foliate scrolls. The dome cover has a finial in the shape of intertwined leaves. Genoa, 1767.

Bottom: Serving dish from Turin, third quarter of the 18th century. The smooth circular body has a dome cover with ribbing and a finial in the shape of a panicle with foliate elements.

integration between the smooth parts and those in relief to create a good compositional balance. The points of attachment where the handles join the body are also important to a stylistic analysis, as is the method employed to achieve the passage from the sculptural form of the finial to the top of the cover. This is an important

Serving dishes

Although based on ancient types, silver serving dishes began to be made during the first half of the 18th century and reached the height of their popularity around the end of that century; they were made only sporadically during the 19th century, and their production ended in the 20th. This type of domestic silver is characteristic of the Mediterranean region: Italy, France and the Iberian peninsula. Most of the Italian examples were made in the central northern area, particularly in the cities of Milan, Genoa, Venice and Turin, where the majority of the most interesting examples were made. Serving dishes were designed to be heated over a flame or coals so that food could be brought to the table hot. Usually round (but oval examples are known), they have two side handles, called wings, which were shaped according to the stylistic trend of the period. The cover has a central finial modelled fancifully in different styles. Some serving dishes are accompanied by a serving tray.

point: in the best models, this passage is achieved gradually, without brusque interruptions. In some pieces, somewhat rare and of impressive overall design, the principal rococo motif spreads from the border of the cover to involve the upper area of the body. This, in turn, is not completely smooth but is gently marked off by undulating ribbing that confers on the whole piece that sense of movement so popular during this stylistic period.

Sugar shakers and bowls

With the remarkable increase in coffee, tea and chocolate drinking during the 18th century came the need to find a sweetener for these beverages that was not sticky like honey or molasses. The solution to this problem came with the arrival in Europe of great quantities of sugar derived from sugarcane. Such sugar had been known and used in Europe since the 16th century, but not in such quanti-

85

Below: Sugar bowl with "ship" cover worked in flowing geometric motifs with finial in the shape of a fruit. Turin, 1759-87.

Bottom: Sugar bowl with dome cover with twisting ribbing. It rests on four feet and has a finial in the shape of a rosebud with leaves. Milan, c. 1790.

ties. Sugar was produced in large cone-shaped cakes, which were broken up into flakes or ground into powder by means of special tongs. Containers for sugar came to be of three different characteristic forms. The first of these is the vertical sugar shaker in the shape of a cylinder or baluster with the upper part perforated to allow the sugar to be shaken out. This model dates from the last quarter of the 17th century and enjoyed a long life, with examples still being made at the beginning of the 20th century. The second model, of a bellied oval form known as a "boat," was made most of all in the Piedmont region of Italy, where it enjoyed particular favour. Because of its shape, this type lent itself well to

the use of rococo stylistic elements. The third model was shaped like a circular bowl with a cover. Sugar containers with the boat-shaped body are of particu-

lar interest. The cover's sense of movement is related to the form itself and is accentuated by bands of decoration using typical rococo motifs, of which leaves and flowers were the most popular. In many cases both the body of the sugar and its cover are equally involved in the usual play of ribbing with twisting, undulating curves. Particular care was given to the decoration, often intensely plastic, of the top of the cover. These include cast decorations of great whimsy, such as rose buds, fruit, bunches of leaves, Oriental figures, birds and sometimes a dog biting a hare. Equal attention was given to the four minuscule feet on which the sugar bowl stands. These were made in two

Below: Two sugar castors from the United States, dating to 1720 and 1760-70. The first is in octagonal section, the second is pear-shaped with an urn knob.

Bottom: Sugar bowl with cover by Myer Myers of New York, c. 1760. The body is chased with rococo decorations, which are repeated on the cover, which has a gadrooned border.

the highest expressions of luxury. Oval in form with gently curving outlines, they offered broad surfaces for decoration. Tureens are composed of a body, with a cover and side handles, that stands on four feet and in many cases has a presentation tray, which also stands on four feet. The oval shape is emphasized by horizontal ribbing that lightens the volume. Examination of the feet of tureens is of great importance when judging their quality. These feet are shaped like leaves that fold in curls and end in a scroll that acts as the actual foot. In the most elaborate examples the rococo leaves rise from the feet and spread in asymmetrical lines across the lower part of the tureen's body. The handles are also very important, especially those in the form of downward-turning curls with decoration that extends to the upper part of the tureen's body. The fami-

basic types of figurations: reversed scrolls with a foliate attachment and highly stylized animal paws.

Circular sugar bowls enjoyed great favour in both North America, where rococo motifs were engraved or slightly embossed and chased on the body, and in England, where the bowl can be seen as a transformation of the early 18th-century sugar container in the form of a box with a cover. Around 1760 sugar containers in the shape of urns appeared in England; these show clear signs of the change in

taste that was gradually leading towards the renewal of forms taken from classical antiquity.

Tureens

Among silver pieces made for use at table, the most prominent item at the height of the 18th century was the soup tureen. These impressive pieces, often made in pairs, were generally used only by prominent and affluent families. With their elaborate decoration, great size and presentation tray, they constituted, together with centerpieces,

ROCOCO

ly coat of arms often appears on the smooth side of the body, particularly on tureens made in England. Such armorial decorations are either engraved or inserted within a chased rococo cartouche. As with other ornate pieces, the terminal part of the cover is decorated with a sculptural element that serves as a knob for lifting the cover. These finials offered silver-smiths the opportunity to give full rein to their imagination, and they drew on the plant and animal world for their inspiration. Among the favoured themes are roses, buds of pomegran-

ROCOCO FEET

Cast and finished with chasing, the feet of rococo silver objects repeat that period's classical stylistic elements and are characterized by extreme technical precision and impeccable plastic rendering. The most common motifs are curls, elaborated in infinite variants; having lost the rigid compositional symmetry that had distinguished earlier models, they acquired a freer line, sinuous and original.

Where the foot meets the body, these curls usually spread in pleasing foliate scrolls that seem to embrace the body. In the case of rounded objects in particular, the foot had

to expand to form a medallion or mask near the attachment in order to offer a broader surface for the attachment and make the fitting stronger. Plant motifs predomi-

nated at the height of the 18th century, but in the neoclassical the models became more sober and symmetrical, decorated with garlands, female heads and palmettes.

88

ates, artichokes, interwoven leaves in bizarre arrangements and stag horns. Ideally, the presentation tray bore the same decorative repertory as the tureen itself, and in the most finely detailed versions the handles of the tray extend upwards on the sides to meet and balance the downward-curling handles of the tureen.

Flatware at the height of the 18th century

The refined manners of the 18th century led to the development of a true "culture of the table," which was expressed in the progressive general use of flatware, in the increasing tendency towards stylistic homogeneity in the patterns of services, and in the increasing number and variety of pieces, which became specialized to serve particular functions.

The traditional table setting made up of knife, spoon and fork was now joined by a series of special utensils that together created the full table service. The yearning for elegance, refinement and "fine dining" was not exhausted by these additions, however, and many people were unwilling to forgo these amenities even when travelling or dining in the open air. To meet these needs travel sets were made in increased numbers with pieces of flatware that could easily be folded and placed in special, often elaborately worked, cases.

The desire for greater functionality also led to the making of small devices designed to save space; among the most refined of such inventions are handles fitted with small inserted containers cleverly concealed beneath movable decoration. There were also many examples of utensils with multiple uses, such as travelling forks fitted with the bowl of a spoon between the prongs.

ROCOCO

Below: Epergne with five baskets by Thomas Pitts, London, 1763. The structure stands on four fringed and foliate supports; the baskets are finely pierced and chased.

Opposite: Candle snuffers on a small boat-shaped stand with gadrooned border standing on four feet. Venice, third quarter 18th century.

circular section of the handle and fixed there with a resin that hardened, strengthening the connection. Although these new techniques made many new forms and variations possible, the most widespread type of handle used during the rococo period remained the pistol handle in its various regional interpretations. What was new was the tendency to render the handle and the blade co-axial; if the spine of the blade deviated from the axis, the construction of the knife was considered unsatisfying. Even so,

The steady movement towards homogeneity in the decoration of the entire set of flatware brought about a tendency to use silver for the handles of knives. This was made possible thanks to advances in the technique of casting perfected by various specialized artisans, including above all the Frenchman Gavet. The new technique made possible the creation of many varied and original forms. Since the knife blade had to be inserted in the silver handle, the artisan was forced to follow a process of assembly that was very different from that employed with spoons and forks. The handles were cast in two identical parts that were then joined; the tang, the extension of the blade that extends into the handle, was inserted in the hollow

The epergne

The epergne is one of the most characteristic pieces of English silver. The earliest known examples date from around 1725, but most were made in the period running from the end of the 18th century up to the Victorian period. The epergne is an elaborate centerpiece consisting of a frame supporting a central bowl or basket around which are arranged four or more smaller baskets, usually removable. These sprawling objects, used to display and serve fruit or sweets, were usually placed at the center of the table in the fashionable homes of the aristocracy. However, the practical side of the epergne was very often overpowered by its decorative character. Epergnes usually stand on four scroll legs ending in small foliate or shell-shaped feet. The type grew in size and complexity, and

during the 1760s and 1770s their design reached the very limits of rococo fantasy, with sinuous shapes and rich decoration that embraced all the typical motifs of the period. The baskets are frequently pierced, and the arms that support them take on capricious and irregular forms. Later, under the influence of the Adam style, the epergne assumed a more austere appearance, with fluted legs ending in balls or hooks and arms bearing small, usually boat-shaped baskets in pierced silver. During the 19th century epergnes were made that support cut-glass bowls rather than the classic baskets. Because they are composed of several pieces, it is very difficult today to find a period epergne, particularly from the 18th century, in its original state.

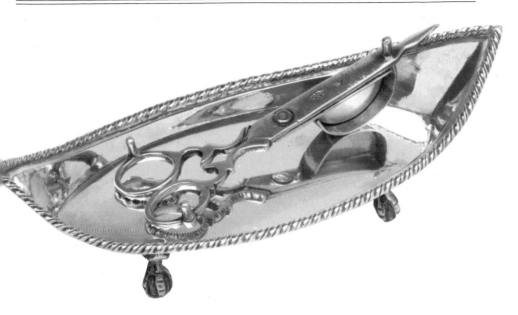

this did not prevent the production of knives with partially curving blades.

Spoons and forks also underwent substantial changes in shape and construction. The reinforcement of the joint between the bowl and stem of the spoon went from the rat-tail type to the "teardrop"; in some cases, primarily in England, this extension ended in a shell motif. New patterns joined those, such as the violin type, in use during the preceding epoch.

Of particular interest was the Onslow pattern, which ends in a shape similar to a scroll or curl. Also widespread was the "olive" type, so-called because the end of the handle spread to form a pronounced oval reminiscent of the shape of an olive. A variant of this model, known as Old English, began in Great Britain and spread through Europe. This has a flat, short handle the end of which curves down or up with slopes forming two faces. Forks were still being

made both with three and four prongs.

Specific types appeared at the regional level. In Scotland and Ireland, the handles of spoons almost always ended in points. The decoration of the handles followed the taste of the period: large foliate scrolls and *rocaille* motifs stand out asymmetrically on the smooth surfaces. In some cases the outline of the end of the handle is itself asymmetrical and takes on a form following the artisan's whim.

FINIALS

At the height of the 18th century, when artisan craft was freed by the decorative fantasies of the rococo, the finial types became more variegated. Those that appeared include foliate scrolls, zoomorphic creations and faithful reproductions of plant elements, whether singly or grouped. The rigour of the neoclassical period brought a predilection for buds, garlands, pinecones and fruit.

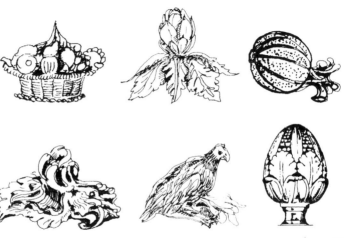

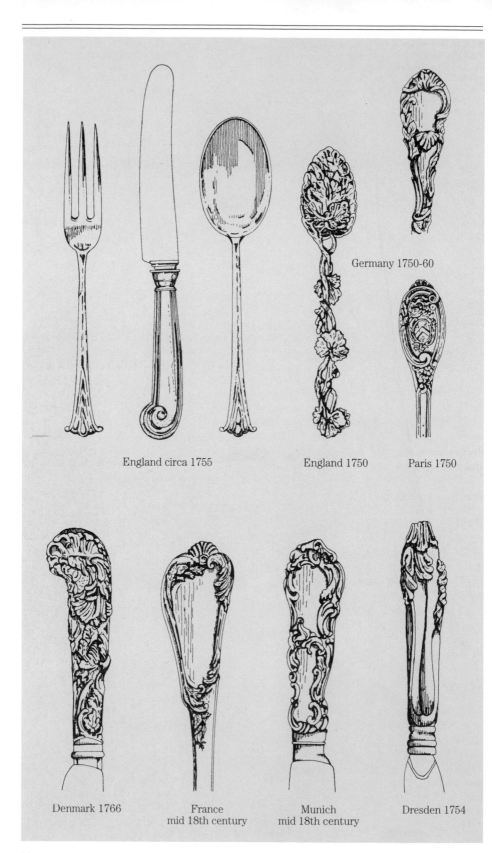

England circa 1755

Germany 1750-60

England 1750

Paris 1750

Denmark 1766

France
mid 18th century

Munich
mid 18th century

Dresden 1754

Below: Coffeepot from Mons (Belgium), 1774. The amphora body is richly decorated with sinuous motifs and festoons that create the sense of a fruit basket.

Below: Coffeepot from Mons (Belgium), 1774. The amphora body is richly decorated with sinuous motifs and festoons that create the sense of a fruit basket.

Bottom: Chocolate pot, Low Countries, end 18th century. The pear-shaped body with twisted ribbing stands on three long feet decorated with motifs that prefigure the neoclassical.

the previous style. Usually referred to as the transition period, this can be said to have lasted a decade, from 1765 to 1775. In general, silver pieces made during this period show a certain hesitant wavering between the curved line and the straight line, and sometimes both lines appear together. Many objects display a structure that has already become rectilinear but is joined to decorations using the stylistic elements of the rococo; many others are intensely curvilinear but bear decorative accents inspired by the classical. The most characteristic element, aside from shape, is the choice of decorative repertory: there is a notable abandonment of floral motifs and the appearance of garlands of laurel, frets, rosettes, ram's heads, lion's paws, festoons and stag horns. This period thus testifies to the contemporaneous existence of two decorative formulas. With some caution, one could say that the field of silver showed the widespread persistence of rococo stylistic elements on forms taken from the classical.

From rococo to neoclassicism

The proliferation, and perhaps also the degeneration, of rococo taste inevitably led to a reaction against it, which began timidly but steadily gained in courage. This repudiation of rococo taste involved a return to symmetry, to models taken from classical antiquity, to a preference (where possible) for straight lines and to a greater restraint in the use of decorative themes. As with all transitional periods, this intermediate style is very hard to date, for it did not suddenly come into being but rather evolved through the ongoing appearance and reappearance of experimental decorative models that did not completely abandon certain formal characteristics of

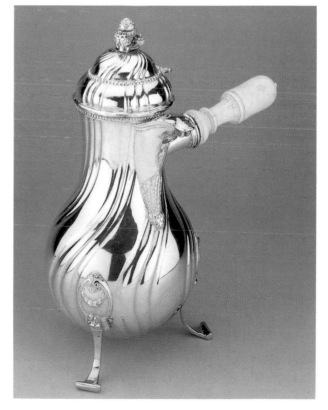

PARISIAN HALLMARKS OF THE 18TH CENTURY

FERMIERS GÈNÈRAUX	DATES IN USE	"CHARGE" MARKS	"DÉCHARGE" MARKS	JURANDE MARKS
VINCENT FORTIER	1672-77			from D to H
J.-B. LUCOT	1677	Three lilies with central A	A crown	I
CHRISTOPHE DE LALIVE	1677	An A over a lily	A crown	
MARTIN DUFRESNOY	1677-80			from K to L
PAUL BRION DU SAUSSOY	1680-88			from M to O
ESTIENNE DE RIDEREAU	1684-87			from P to R
JACQUES LÉGER	1687-91			from R to X
PIERRE POINTAU	1691-98			from Y to D
PIERRE PERRINE	1698-1703			from E to I
ETIENNE BALIGNY	1703-8			from K to O
FLORENT SOLLIER	1708-15			from P to X
PAUL MANIS	1715-17			from Y to Z
ETIENNE DE BOUGES CHARLES VYON ARMAND PILLAVOINE	1717-22			from A to E
CHARLES CORDIER	1722-26			from F to I
JACQUES COTTIN LOUIS GERVAIS	1726-32			from K to Q
HUBERT LOUVET	1732-38			from R to X

FERMIERS GÈNÈRAUX	DATES IN USE	"CHARGE" MARKS	"DÉCHARGE" MARKS	JURANDE MARKS
LOUIS ROBIN	1738-44			from Y to C
ANTOINE LESCAUDEL	1744-50			from D to I
JULIEN BERTHE	1750-56	An ox head		from K to P
ELOY BRICHARD	1756-62			from Q to X
JEAN-JACQUES PRÉVOST	1762-68			from Y to D
JULIENNE ALATERRE	1768-74			from E to K
JEAN-BAPTISTE FOUACHE DOMINIQUE COMPANT	1774-80			from L to Q
				from R to U
HENRI CLAVEL	1780-89			
J.F. KALANDRIN	1789			

SEVERAL 18TH-CENTURY HALLMARKS

Iberian Peninsula

LISBON

1720   1730   1730   1780   1782   end 18th cent.

COIMBRA

18th cent.

OPORTO

1758-78   1778-92   1792-1810   end 18th cent.

SETÚBAL

18th cent.

ÉVORA

18th cent.

GUIMARÃES

end 18th cent.

MADRID

1794   1797   end 18th cent.

BARCELONA

18th cent.

LEÓN   **ÁVILA**

1732   18th cent.

CÁCERES

end 17th-18th cent.

NEOCLASSICISM

Below: Sugar bowl with cover, Turin, end 18th century. The boat-shaped body, decorated with fluting and beading, stands on four shaped feet.

Italian contributions to the neoclassical style

The large-scale return to classical antiquity brought Italy to the front ranks for the simple reason that it is the European country with the highest concentration of ancient architecture. Much has been said about the influence on the applied arts of the archaeological finds from excavations at Herculaneum, Pompeii and other centers in Campania during the 1740s and 1750s. Without doubt the news of these discoveries resounded throughout the world, but the rulers of Naples jealously guarded the privacy of the sites. Few foreigners were permitted to visit the excavations, and making sketches at the sites was absolutely forbidden. As a result, the decorations of Herculaneum and Pompeii did not have a determining influ-

ence during the 18th century; what did were descriptions of Roman, Greek and Egyptian antiquity. Silversmiths, in search of decorative models through which to express themselves in the new neoclassical style, were helped most by the decorative works of Giovanni Battista Piranesi (1720-78) in the Roman area and those of Giocondo Albertolli

(1742-1839) in the areas of Emilia and Lombardy. There was also the contribution of the multi-talented Luigi Valadier (1726-85), a Roman of French origin. Even if not directly tied to the subject of silver, these artists, seen in the broadest sense as creators of models, offered such a large quantity of decorative details that silversmiths had a constant

Opposite bottom left:
Sugar bowl by Carlo
Mariano, Turin, 1778-
96, decorated with
bands of stylized
arabesques and small
fluting; the finial is
shaped like a melon.

Opposite bottom right:
Sugar bowl with a
convex body decorated
with shell motifs and
divided into sections
with cover with bud-
shaped finial. Turin,
end 18th century.

Below: Set of four
casseroles by Antoine
Dutry, Paris, 1770-71.
The smooth circular
bodies have dome covers
with finials shaped like
artichokes with open
leaves.

and abundant supply of neoclassical motifs.

Models from Piranesi, Albertolli and Valadier

The engraver and architect Giovanni Battista Piranesi was born in the Veneto region but spent the greater part of his life in Rome, where he made engravings of the buildings and monuments of the ancient city. He was deeply interested in these ruins of antiquity and translated them into exceptionally detailed engravings.

His interest in antiquity led him to publish two volumes of engravings of ancient decorations in which reality blends wonderfully with fancy and romance. The first of these, known as *Diverse Maniere* ("Different Ways"; the full title trans-

HALLMARKS OF PIEDMONTESE SILVERSMITHS

Until 1793, the hallmarks used by Piedmontese silversmiths were regulated by a directive issued in 1678 by Maria Giovanna Battista, regent of the Savoy States, that prohibited the making or sale of silver objects of a standard beneath eleven deniers (equal to 916.667 parts fine silver). Aside from the obligation of affixing

Giovanni Battista Bollea (1771-93)

Pietro Cebrano (1726-?)

Carlo Mariano (1786-1824)

Bartolomeo Bernardi (1778-1816)

the hallmark of the master silversmith, this law also imposed the necessity of an assay with the addition of the assayer's mark, the crowned coat of arms of Savoy usually flanked by the assayer's initials. To further protect buyers, a second assay, called the counterassay, was required, and this was indicated by a further hallmark, oval with a beaded border enclosing the marks of the counterassayer.

NEOCLASSICISM

lates as "Different Ways of Decorating Fireplaces and Every Other Part of Buildings") and based on Egyptian, Etruscan, Greek and Roman architecture, was published in 1769; Piranesi was in the habit of selling his prints individually, however, as he completed them and before they were published, which explains how many neoclas-

sical decorative models came to be made before 1769. The second work, known as *Vasi, Candelabri, Cippi* ("Vases, Candelabra, Pillars"), also deals with antique ornaments; composed of 110 engraved plates, it was published in 1778 and is the work that drew the most attention from Roman silversmiths of the late 18th century.

The fund of decorative motifs supplied by Piranesi's engravings include all those that belong to the lexicon of neoclassical taste. Those most often repeated in silverwork are cornucopias, panoplies, masks, vases, rosettes, obelisks, urns, palmettes, helmets, garlands of flowers or leaves, plant volutes, vines, laurel wreaths, acanthus leaves, seashells, satyrs, bacchants, dancers, flautists, tritons, cupids, Medusa heads, eagles, lions, ram heads, deer, as well as a wide choice of sphinxes, male and female and with or without wings.

The influence of Piranesi's daring ornamental extravagances shows up in Roman silvers primarily in pieces of great decorative flair; these can be compared to the restraint and severity of Giocondo Albertolli's designs, which had a not-

THE BORDERS OF ENGLISH PLATES AND SALVERS

Study of the ornamental motifs and finishing of the borders on plates and salvers can be useful in the analysis of a given piece and can help establish the date of manufacture. Shown here are the most common borders of English silver, with indications of the periods when each was particularly popular; many motifs were repeated either

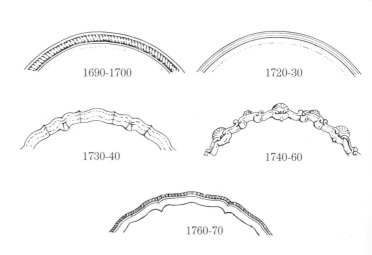

1690-1700

1720-30

1730-40

1740-60

1760-70

Tureen with serving plate by Giuseppe and Luigi Valadier, Rome, c. 1780. The oval body rests on four lion-paw feet and bears a decorative strip with classical motifs of so-called Vitruvian waves; on the sides, lion-head masks bear rings in their mouths as handles. On the central pedestal mounting of the cover stands a finial with the sculptural figure of a child with basket.

ations, Invented, Designed, and Drawn by Giocondo Albertolli (1782) and *Decorations of Noble Halls* (1787). Among the many stylistic elements of the rigorous neoclassicism he introduced stand out the volutes of acanthus leaves, friezes decorated with medallions, rosettes and, among animals, dolphins and eagles.

Like Piranesi, both Petitot and Albertolli were architects, but not goldsmiths. The professional experience of Luigi Valadier was quite different. He was a silversmith, goldsmith, foundryman, mounter of cameos, and worked variously in stone as well as in iron and brass; he also had experience as a cabinetmaker. His Roman workshop was protected by Pope Pius VI, for whom he was "superintendent of restorations of ancient bronzes and mounter of cameos to the two sacred

able influence on the neoclassical silver of Lombardy. Albertolli was born in the Ticino but educated in Parma, where he was influenced by the French architect Edmond-Alexandre Petitot (1727-1801), leading exponent of the neoclassical in Parma and author of a book of patterns (*Suite de Vases*), published in 1764. Albertolli became a teacher of decoration at the Brera Academy in 1774 and was an important source of designs and decorations, an activity that led to his publishing two volumes of engravings: *Various Decor-*

entirely or in altered reinterpretations, particularly during the second half of the 19th century and even for a good part of our century. One of the most widespread methods from the end of the 17th century on was gadrooning, continuous series of lobes and fluting, usually curved, that permitted the creation of numerous variations and that was particularly well-suited to the decoration of borders.

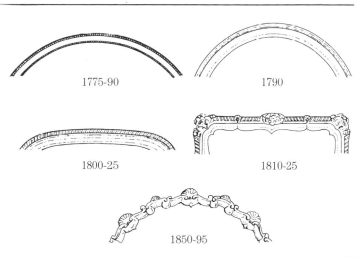

1775-90

1790

1800-25

1810-25

1850-95

NEOCLASSICISM

and profane museums," and his clientele was of the upper rank. As a result, his production in the field of silver was of the highest quality and was so popular that he had a large number of imitators. His expression of the neoclassical, however, is almost always marked by Renaissance and late baroque memories. In fact, living and working in Rome, in the presence of examples from past centuries, it was difficult to free oneself from these influences. Thus the presence of curling acanthus leaves and the insistent use of gadrooning are remi-

niscent of Renaissance models, while his predilection for paired scrolls indicates the force of the late baroque. His work was carried on by his son Giuseppe (1762-1839), silversmith to the Vatican, director of the Vatican foundry and, from 1786, also an architect. Giuseppe's fame rests primarily on his being one of the leading exponents of Italian neoclassicism in architecture; however, his familiarity with designs and his activities as director of his father's workshop also made him a point of reference for Roman silversmiths. Piedmontese silversmiths display equal measures of influence from both their Roman colleagues and from those in nearby France.

Neoclassical candlesticks and candelabra

The production of silver for lighting experienced a notable impulse during the neoclassical period in part because of the expansion of the areas of domestic life. In addition to dining rooms, there were now desks, library tables, toilets, bedside tables, fireplaces and consoles to illuminate, as well as the areas used for polite conversation and those set aside specifically for drinking tea or coffee. The candlesticks made can

be divided into two basic models. the baluster-stemmed model and the column model. The baluster type had a small square base plate with slight gadrooned decoration, or was polylobate with the stem rising from a bell-shaped base. The stem is of the baluster type with some flaring and one or two projecting knots;

or it is in polygonal section and has a garland at a high spot that falls back and softens the whole. In simpler examples the stem, slender and almost without decoration, is in the shape of a small column with a swelling in the lower area. The flaring base rises from a plate that comes to assume a round shape. In a certain sense, the column type repeats the models of the late 17th century, but with a greater thinness, which results from the vertical thrust of the stem, which is really a column of Corinthian or Composite order with a fluted body. In these types, it is the capital of the column that serves as the socket for the candle. In this sense, there is no break in the continuity between base, column and capital. Candelabra almost always have the baluster-type stem, and a typically neoclassical decorative motif is located at the top of the stem, above the point were the two arms meet. The arms are styled as

NEOCLASSICISM

*Below: Pair of salt cellars, Brescia, last quarter 18th century.
The oval bodies, entirely pierced with geometric motifs, rest on four ribbed feet.*

Bottom: Pair of double salt cellars by Robert-Joseph Auguste, Paris, 1768. Each is composed of a pair of cupids kneeling before shell bowls and supporting on their backs a covered vase.

foliate scrolls and initially were somewhat short, later taking the form of a long, wide S. The base is almost always round, and the decoration is in perfect accord with the rest of the piece. Candelabra differed from simple two-branched candlesticks primarily in terms of size and for the presence of an urn located above the stem. In some cases the stem is a fluted column without capital and is decorated with garlands; applied to it is an ovoid form from which the arms spread. The sockets of candelabra are always impressive, and the small plate to catch wax is located not near the top but towards the base. In this arrangement, the socket with the plate beneath it resembles a flower bud with its leaves, but without a single concession to naturalistic realism.

French neoclassicism, or the Louis XVI style

The redirection of style that led from the rococo to neoclassicism was fuelled in

rather sensed as a source of inspiration for research into harmony and proportion, or as a rich decorative repertory to be treated with the same freedom as the rococo treated its preferred motifs.

In this regard, analysis of the forms reveals a growing marriage between decorative elements taken from classical antiquity and cle

part by a desire to go from almost total inventive liberty to intense levels of sobriety and regularity.

The relationship between the so-called Louis XVI style and that of his immediate predecessor does not appear in any sense antithetical. Although the fundamental tenets of the French neoclassical style—from the triumph of the pure line to the reduction of decorative elements and the return to classical antiquity—move in a direction that differs with the basic trends

of the rococo, the way in which these new elements were treated by silversmiths was extremely similar to the spirit of the earlier style Louis XVI neoclassicism is constantly animated by a desire for lightness and movement, without any of the concessions to grandiose and monumental inspiration typical of the classicism of the late baroque of the period of Louis XIV.

Classical antiquity is almost never used as a "model" in the rigid sense in these new works, but is

The dish cross

The first examples of the food warmer known as the dish cross date from about 1735, although most examples were made between 1755 and 1780. Of English origin, it is composed of two pairs of arms of square section hinged to a central body (so they can be moved to accommodate the shape of the plate) bearing a spirit burner. The arms stand on adjustable shaped feet and have extended supports, also shaped, on which the plate rests.

NEOCLASSICISM

ments of fantasy. In many senses, this imitation of antiquity is the essential element for an understanding of this new style, although it does not explain every aspect of the style. From this point of view one can see with greater clarity how certain aspects of this style make it part of the ambience of profound cultural renewal that culminated in the Enlightenment and the revolution but also how this style was an important fashion movement. This was the double sense in which French society took the order to "return to the ancient."

Aspects of the style that are typical of a fashion movement include the extreme speed with which the new style was embraced. Upper-class French society in the 18th century loved to keep up with the times, hated what had become "old," and enthusiastically pursued this new stylistic adventure.

The creators of French neoclassical decorative models

The climate of stylistic renewal in France or, more accurately, in Paris was affected directly by important contributions from many artists. The many books of engravings of ornamental models affected silver only indirectly, but silversmiths found much inspiration for a change in their stylistic expression in the details provided by the themes and motifs dear to neoclassicism, both in terms of sculptural forms and in terms of pure ornament. The panorama is broad: from the *Recueil de Griffonis* by the abbot Saint-Non, published in the years 1771-74, to the impressive series by Delafosse and Neufforge, Forty and Salembier. Richard Lalonde, an important point of reference in the second half of the 18th century, was quite prolific with the production of some eighty collections, most of all the work *Oeuvres Diverses de Lalonde, Decorateur et Dessinateur*,

THE DECORATION OF BORDERS
The decoration of borders was enriched by new, original models during the neoclassical period. Based on classical antiquity, but reexamined and subjected to free interpretation, these led to sober and elegant continuous motifs, including rows of laurel leaves and berries bound by ribbons, frets hung with festoons, stylized rosettes within frames and "Vitruvian waves."

the subtitle of which promised "a great number of designs for decoration."

Lalonde was principally an engraver and designer of ornaments; Jean-Charles Delafosse (1734-89) was an architect and leading expert on geometric designs and perspective, and his models, in forty series, reveal the compositional rigour typical of designers.

A contribution not yet studied was given by the 900 engravings in the celebrated *Recueil Elémentaire d'Architecture*, which appeared between 1757 and 1772 and was the work of the sculptor, engraver and architect Jean François de Neufforge (1714-91). Although this work is dedicated primarily to architectural plans and rooms, the section on "details" presents such a broad selection of neoclassical stylistic elements that it constitutes a well of highly stimulating decorative models. In the panorama of creators of models related to silver, there was also the Parisian Jean François Forty, who dedicated himself entirely to the production of models for works in metal.

The most important creator of French neoclassical models was Henry Salem-

bier (or Sallembier or Sallambier), who lived between about 1753 and 1810. The thirty collections of decorative models he produced present images of extreme precision and complexity, the product of a particularly fine and incisive line with motifs of such subtle lightness they seem almost threadlike. Salembier made an important contribution to the refinement of the final period of French neoclassicism. Lightness and movement seem to have been the constant aspirations of his fertile and whimsical imagination, as presented in designs as charming as they are complex. French silversmiths of this period were indebted to all these designers, who put at their disposal a wealth of books of decorative models. The silversmiths them-

NEOCLASSICISM

*Below left: Coffeepot
made in Bruges in 1787.
The spout is close
against the neck of the
pear-shaped body and
is decorated with a
female head. The finial
is a seated putto with
cornucopia.*

*Below right: Coffeepot
in gilt silver made in
Brussels in 1785. The
body, animated by con-
tinuous vertical fluting,
stands on three curling
feet.*

selves, especially those who
were most well known, prepared their own designs.
These were working mod-
els, however, and thus were
stored in the workshop or
store and were worn out
through constant use,
which explains why few
traces of these remain.

The proliferation of
English silver

The second half of the 18th
century saw the multiplica-
tion of types of silver pieces
for the table and for enter-

taining in general. The new
types, added to the many
that had already been in use
for years, included the small
vessel shaped like a cof-
feepot but used to keep
gravy warm at table known
as the argyll, breakfast
plates with covers and heat-
ing stands to keep food
warm during the traditionally large English cooked
breakfast, containers for
butter with the covers decorated with a cow, caddy
spoons for scooping tea
leaves, coasters used under
bottles, various creamers,

domed dish covers for keeping food warm, containers
for honey in the shape of
hives, mustard pots and
wine coolers.

The large amount of silver
available in England can be
partially explained by the
fact that the Industrial
Revolution was gathering
pace in England. The small
artisan workshop composed
of master silversmith, helper
and several workers had
given way to the first facto-
ries set up on an industrial
level. The pieces of highest
quality were still made indi-

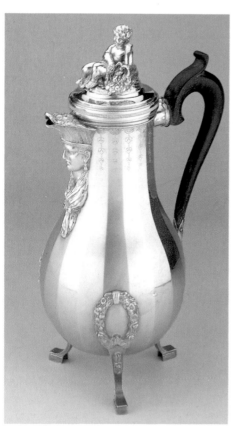
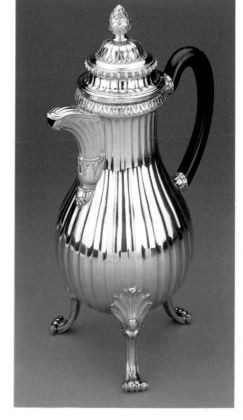

Coffeepot made in Malta between 1798 and 1800. The pear-shaped body stands on three animal-hoof feet and has a finial shaped like an Oriental figure.

object from a flat sheet of silver; the parts were then assembled by hand. The gradual movement towards mass production was given great impulse by the steam engine, invented by Matthew Boulton. The machine in his factory in Birmingham made pieces of silver plate that were then sold to small companies of silversmiths who saw to the mounting and to the addition of suitable decoration.

The formal and decorative simplicity of the neoclassical style contributed in large measure to the expansion of mass industrial production. Around the end of the century, low-priced silver pieces began to be made in Sheffield and Birmingham. At that time, many London silversmiths started to sell silver made in the industrial areas of Birmingham and Sheffield along with their own production.

vidually by hand, but ordinary, less formal pieces could be made in series, and recourse was made to special machines that could mechanically reproduce the processes of embossing, casting and piercing.

As early as 1769 a press had been invented that was capable of cutting and punching pieces for an

As a result of the emergence of these important centers of production, the silver trade in England had to be reorganized with new regulations and new hallmarks for the assay offices.

Exportation is another important factor. London silversmiths had long been exporting their wares to the American colonies; this trade was interrupted by the American Revolution, but with the recognition of American independence in 1783, this exportation resumed with increased vigour.

Thanks to this increased production, English wrought plate was also exported to the countries of Europe, particularly Portugal, Spain, Denmark and Sweden. These exported pieces influenced local silversmiths. Although on a small scale, the influence of English silver can be noted even

THE NEOCLASSICAL DECORATIVE REPERTORY

Most of the decorative motifs that appeared on silver objects made during the last thirty years of the 18th century were based on models from classical antiquity. This influence is undeniable, but it is also true that the ancient models were never slavishly copied, but were rather taken as the starting point for the elaboration of a new

ornamental language arranged to create a harmonious whole, at the same time elegant, sober and rigorous. Plant elements, so often used in the preceding period, were used in the neoclassical period, but radically reworked and reinterpreted: rosettes, oak fronds, acanthus leaves, palmettes and rose vines are characterized by a rigorous symmetry and by an extreme precision of design, subtle and incisive.

NEOCLASSICISM

among the highly skilled artisans of Paris and can be explained by the fact that the signing of the commercial treaty in 1786 permitted the exportation of English silver even to France.

Robert Adam

The architect Robert Adam (1728-92) is internationally recognized as the father of the classic revival, the outgrowth of the English neoclassical that came to be developed during the period of George III, to whom Adam was architect from 1762 to 1768, when he was succeeded by his brother James. Passionately interested in antique art, Adam had studied in Rome, where he befriended Piranesi. He

travelled in Dalmatia and Greece, and following the clamorous response to the archaeological excavations at Pompeii and Herculaneum he dedicated himself to bringing back the forms of classical antiquity. Particularly important was his study *Ruins of the Palace of the Emperor Diocletian at Spalatro in Dalmatia* (1764).

At the same time, the architects James Stuart and Nicolas Revett spent four years in Athens and then published their *Antiquities*. They were fanatical Hellenists, and their work came to participate in a heated debate on the supremacy of the arts: which is closer to artistic perfection, Hellenic art or Roman? Adam, however, was too original and independent to take a clear position in the debate: although he accepted the traditional Palladian elements, his style also showed his studies in both the Greek and Roman worlds, so much so that in substance his was a completely autonomous and personal style.

His originality and the fact that in addition to being an architect, he was also a decorator and designer of furniture and decorative models, led to his having much influence not only in architecture but also in the entire field related to the applied arts in the last

forty years of the 18th century. As a decorator, he did not overlook the works of his French colleagues, nor did he forget the works of the Renaissance masters. His decorative repertory presents a vast gamut of motifs, and of these those inspired by Roman and Etruscan antiquities were taken up in the works of English silversmiths.

These motifs include heads of goats, griffins, sphinxes, festoons of flowers, knotted ribbons, elongated amphoras, cameos, griffins with garlands and palmettes, paired spirals with falling drapery, but most of all certain decorative motifs of which he was particularly fond, including a particular semicircular motif called the open umbrella and garlands of bellflowers and honeysuckle. Because of his intense activity as an architect and decorator and thanks also to his collaboration with his brother James, his works became enormously famous and spread his influence from his homeland to northern Europe, Russia and America.

FESTOONS

Festoons were one of the most popular motifs in English silver of the neoclassical period. Much of their popularity resulted from the works of the architect Robert Adam, who designed a great number of ornamental models that had a vast influence in the field of decorative and applied arts in Great Britain. Festoons were widespread and were presented in infinite variations.

NEOCLASSICISM

Below: Tureen by Garbiel Marcello Giuliano, Turin, 1787-93. The upper border is decorated with a motif of reeds held by ribbons. The final is in the shape of a cabbage and artichoke.

Bottom: One of a pair of tureens by Berthold Christian Schlepper, St. Petersburg, 1774. The tureen stands on an oval tray by Antoine Boullier, Paris, 1780.

Tureens as centerpieces

Among the wide variety of pieces of silver that decorated the table of the neoclassical period there was one whose size, decoration and elaborate execution attracted the most attention, becoming, once laid on the table, the centerpiece of any setting: this was the tureen. The monumental nature of tureens was well suited to the pomp of the decorative repertory of neoclassical style. Since it has a server, a tray slightly raised on almost hidden feet, the tureen assumes the same importance as an elaborate centerpiece. The large round body is well suited to taking both the typical decoration of gadrooning and the more complex decora-

tion of garlands and festoons. Silversmiths also paid great attention to the side handles and the tri-

umphal finial of the cover. As for the handles, lion or ram heads were preferred for the ring-bearing masks; more rarely seen are coiled snakes. But it is the sculptural decoration of the cover that lifted the tureen to the highest points of inventive fantasy. It was in sculpture that the finest silversmiths excelled themselves. The most common, and invariably somewhat complex, model took the form of a pine. The representations of human figures in relaxed poses are striking for their essential nature, while the scenes dedicated to wild beasts fallen to the blows of hunters or of dogs retrieving game led to the world of realistic representation

Tureen with tray made in Vienna, 1777. The cover bears a sculptural group of a hunting scene, with dog, hares, haversack and tree trunk.

that met with great favour in pieces from the 19th century. When examining the formal characteristics of a tureen, it is important to note the congruence, both formal and decorative, of the feet that support it, for these must be in accord with the rest and must participate discreetly in the general lines of the whole. These feet are usually shaped like reversed volutes, the most suitable shape for expanding the surface of support of the tureen. Also, more rarely seen, are feet in the form of fluted pilasters that reach up to the middle of the body and thus are a prelude to models of the Empire style.

Flatware of the neoclassical period

The height of the 18th century saw the progressive affirmation of the "culture of the table," a gradual refinement of dining customs; by the final thirty years of the century, this trend had undergone a radical change in the sense that it had extended from the court and aristocratic circles to affect even the less well-to-do classes. By then, the use of flatware had become general, and the fork was appearing on all tables, including those of the middle class and the common people. The process of specialization of flatware that had led to the appearance of special utensils designed to meet increasingly precise and particular needs continued and, in fact, intensified. Coffee spoons, ice cream spoons with flat bowls shaped like spatulas, sugar spoons with finely pierced bowls, salt spoons and ladles, corkscrews and other table accessories began making their appearance as additions to the

NEOCLASSICISM

classic table setting. Silver was still used for all important table services and its position was unchallenged; services made with pieces in other materials, such as porcelain, crystal, mother of pearl, or glass, were completely abandoned, in part because the new style demanded a certain formal and decorative rigour best served by silver. The most striking changes in shape and type affected the knife. The typical pistol-grip handle and long curved blade with rounded point, so popular in preceding years, were finally abandoned. The handle was now given an oval section with parallel sides or sides slightly tapering towards the blade and with a roundish back to the

handle. The blade, too, underwent an evolution, being made in extremely thin metal and becoming more tapered, narrower, and with its back along the axis of the handle and generally straight. In some cases the upper border and the cutting edge join to form a point, although never in a pronounced manner. The blade was tempered, ground, sharpened and finally bur-

nished; the cutting edge was maintained by being rubbed along a piece of willow four centimeters wide and about forty long spread with sand.

Knives went through a marked evolution during this period, but the same cannot be said for the other two pieces that comprise the individual table setting, the spoon and fork. The three-pronged fork was finally abandoned completely in favour of the four-pronged version; and almost all examples from the period have a teardrop-shaped moulding in place of rat tails near the juncture with the handle. The most popular patterns of handles were those inherited from the preceding period, in particular the violin shape in its various versions, the fillet, the Old English, and the Fiddle Thread, which the French called the *filet-accolade* since the outline of the handle is not straight but spreads out in curves to form a pronounced roundish head. This persistence of models

Opposite top: Tureen by Luigi Leone, Milan, between the 18th and 19th centuries. The oval embossed silver body is gadrooned and stands on curled feet; the handles are rams' heads.

Opposite bottom: Tureen by Carlo Bortolotti, Rome, 1780-90. The oval body stands on four embossed hermae. The handles are formed of the elongated horns of two rams' heads.

Below: Tureen with cover and tray by Jacques-Charles Mongenot, Paris, 1783-84. The body rests on four mermaids with forked tails and has a spread-wing eagle for finial.

handed down from 18th-century tradition was accompanied by radical stylistic-decorative revisions. First of all, the tendency towards homogeneity among all the various pieces of flatware was consolidated; in particular, the knife, which for reasons of its construction had always presented at least minor differences, was successfully brought into complete harmony with the fork and spoon. The decoration returned to that dominated by rigid symmetry, with well defined outlines and without any concessions to the creative fancies that characterized many examples from the rococo period. The motifs used most often were those characteristic of the neoclassical period, in particular garlands, ribbons and continuous beading. The English showed particular

fondness for a type based on models by Adam that was distinguished by great linear simplicity; the only concession to decoration was, in fact, a series of vertical parallel lines alternating with smooth sections.

NEOCLASSICAL DECORATIVE MOTIFS

In part as a reaction to the excesses occasionally reached during the late rococo, the decoration of neoclassical silver was more rigorous and calligraphic, with a return to the domination of rigid symmetry. Cupids, urns, garlands, crowns, flames, rows of pearls, frets, drapery with cords and folds, medallions, laurel crowns and trophies are among the most popular themes.

The traits that most distinguished these motifs were lightness and extreme precision and complexity of line, which permitted them to harmonize with the sober forms of the silver of the period. The often exhaustive collections of patterns assembled by the decorators of the period proved great sources of inspiration.

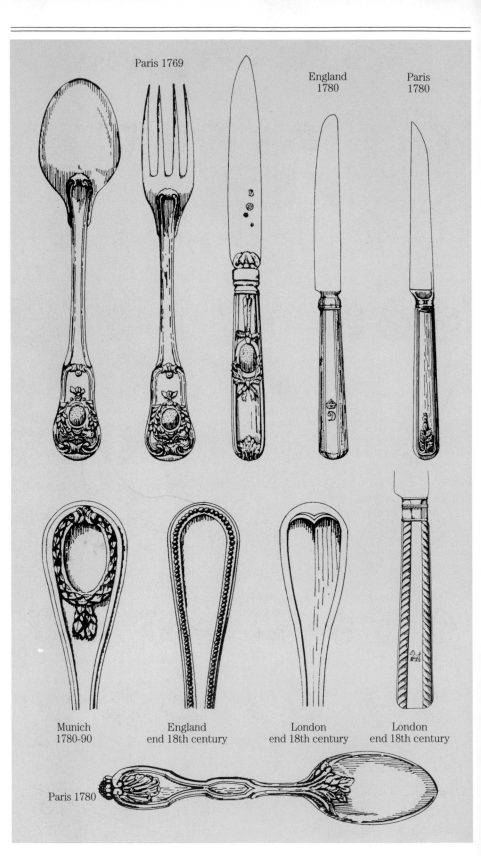

Paris 1769

England 1780

Paris 1780

Munich
1780-90

England
end 18th century

London
end 18th century

London
end 18th century

Paris 1780

SEVERAL 18TH-CENTURY HALLMARKS
Italy

ROME	PARMA	NAPLES

| 1720-60 | end 18th cent. | 18th cent. | 18th cent. | 1716 | 1720 | 1782 |

FERRARA	BOLOGNA	MANTUA	SYRACUSE	PALERMO	RAGUSA	FLORENCE

| 18th cent. | 18th cent. | 18th cent. | 18th cent. | 18th cent. | 18th cent. | 17th-18th cent. |

TRIESTE	TURIN	LUCCA

11 ounces   10 ounces

| end 18th cent. | 1678-1792 | end 18th cent. | 1743-1801 |

German-language Countries

ALTONA	AUGSBURG	BERLIN

| 1748 | 1736 | 1753-55 | 1769-71 | early 18th cent | 1735 | mid 18th cent. |

DRESDEN	DÜSSELDORF	FRANKFURT

| early 18th cent. | 1739 | mid 18th cent. | 18th cent. | early 18th cent. | mid 18th cent. | end 18th cent. |

HAMBURG	HANOVER	CONSTANCE	VIENNA

| 1711 | 1737 | 1762 | 1726 | 18th cent. | 1719 | 1776 |

LEIPZIG	MAINZ	STUTTGART	BASEL

| early 18th cent. | 18th cent. | 1719 | 1761 | 1700-60 | 18th cent. |

LÜBECK	NUREMBERG	RATISBON	POTSDAM	BUDAPEST

| 18th cent. | end 18th cent. | 18th cent. | 18th cent. | 1775 |

SEVERAL 18TH-CENTURY HALLMARKS

Scandinavian Countries

COPENHAGEN

1721   1725   1733   1758

LINKÖPING

end 18th cent.

ODENSE

1763   1725

AALBORG

1717   1745

STOCKHOLM

17th-18th cent.

BERGEN

1781   1753   1767

LULEÅ

18th cent.

LUND

18th cent.

KALMAR

18th cent.

ARBOGA

between 17th and 18th cent.

HEDMARK

18th cent.

Low Countries

AMSTERDAM

18th cent.

UTRECHT

1710   18th cent.

HAARLEM

18th cent.

ROTTERDAM

18th cent.

ANTWERP

1711-12   1734-35   1738

TOURNAI

1737   1752   1786

BRUSSELS

early 18th cent.   1724   1751

LIÈGE

1704   1711   1725   1772

GHENT

first half 18th cent.   1776

19TH-CENTURY SILVER

Empire
Regency
Restoration
Eclecticism

EMPIRE

Right: One of a pair of candlesticks by Shore & Rotheram, Sheffield, 1801-2. The stem rises from a gadrooned base and ends in the form of a feathered capital.

The birth of French Empire silver

The dramatic events of French history during the closing years of the 18th century had an inevitable impact on the arts in general and in particular on the development of silver. Throughout the entire 18th century, the monarchy and its court circles played the dominant role in every form of artistic expression. The sudden loss of this all-important sponsor of the arts, along with the economic and social difficulties that beset the country following the revolution, brought to a complete halt

the production of silver in the styles of the *ancien régime*. Indeed, a great many objects made during the previous years, looked upon with contempt as symbols of the hated and accursed aristocracy, were taken into exile, sold, or even melted down. According to a rough but plausible calculation, as many as fifty-four tons of silver objects were destroyed in just two years, 1789 and 1790. Finally free of the oppression of fear, the country entered the period of the Directory (1795-99), during which secular silver slowly returned to life, fed by the new society's growing taste for pleasantries and luxury. The works from this period are repetitions of the Louis XVI style; indeed, some are entire copies of the last models of Salembier. Their forms are slender and elongated, and their uninventive decoration is a slavish repetition of tried and tested designs from the neoclassical repertory.

Napoleon Bonaparte's arrival on the political scene inaugurated a new era that, as well as making an indelible mark on the historical events of Europe during the early 19th century, also brought its influence to bear on every creative activity. It was clear as early as the Consulate period (1799-1804) that the future emperor was dedicated to

returning France to the splendours it had not known since the death of Louis XIV. Every form of artistic expression was affected; either directly by Napoleon or by the group of men to whom he had entrusted responsibility for establishing the dictates of the new style—the government architects Charles Percier (1764-1838) and Pierre François Fontaine (1762-1853) and the painters Jacques-Louis David (1748-1825) and Pierre Paul Prud'hon (1758-1823), both pairs of artists enthralled by the models of classical antiquity. The production of silver flourished under the state's new centralized and authoritarian form of government, which contributed decisively to the exceptional stylistic uniformity of artistic creations during the Empire period.

Napoleon's role and the new art sponsors

During the years immediately following the revolution, the art of metalworking fell into a depressed state in France with no hope of relief in sight; but by the end of the Empire period, this situation had changed radically.

The preface to a collection of silver presented at the *Exposition des Produits de l'Industrie Française* in

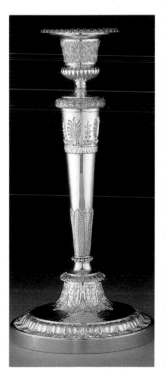

1819 states, "Over the past twenty years the French goldsmith trade expanded in such an extraordinary way and has achieved such levels of perfection that it can hardly be matched. Therefore, no king in Europe, no prince or rich individual would hesitate today to place an order in France."

There is no doubt that Napoleon himself contributed directly to this extraordinary and sudden rebirth of silver production, for he looked on every form of artistic expression as an effective instrument of propaganda, capable, if properly guided and rigidly controlled, of exalting the greatness and power of both the new regime and the man who stood at its head. With the double aim of regenerating industry and commerce and reconstructing around himself a magnificence similar to that of the former royal courts, Bonaparte acted directly, both as first consul and, most of all, as emperor, through a series of important commissions to factories and artisans. Among these, obviously, were many silversmiths.

Always a symbol of wealth and pomp, silver and especially vermeil, which enjoys a prestige almost equal to that of gold, was made in great quantities to embellish every area of the imperial palaces. Impressive show pieces stood out on elegant dining

tables, including triumphs, tureens, cups and candelabra of monumental size. The empress Josephine, who was as fond of luxury as the emperor, commissioned the creation of numerous works in silver for her personal use: aside from many toilet services there was a precious tea and coffee service made especially for her by Auguste and Odiot. The new French aristocracy conformed to Napoleon's stylistic dictates and, following the emperor's lead, rushed to place immense orders with the most celebrated Parisian silversmiths.

The innovative aspect of all this was the appearance

of a new, far larger public, composed of the members of the revolutionary middle class. The process of democratization of the clientele, already underway during the period of the reign of Louis XVI, increased steadily, and the lowering of prices that resulted from the increasingly abundant production and the progressive passage during this period from artisanal work to a proto-industrial stage facilitated the transition. The artisans of Paris, who worked something like forty tons of rough metal each year, found themselves dealing increasingly with the middle class.

An important aspect of the French imperial economy was the exportation of works in silver: nearly three quarters of the national production crossed France's borders, destined to decorate and enrich halls of the courts of half Europe, in particular those of Russia, Bavaria and Austria.

The suppression of guilds and the quality of silver

During the Empire period, the production and commercialization of French silver was regulated by laws that had been passed during both the revolutionary and Directory periods. In 1791 and 1797, with two successive laws, the guilds were suppressed and the system of 18th-century hallmarks, by then obsolete and overtaken by events, was revised in an integral way. The suppression of the old guilds opened a new chapter in the production of silver in France.

Anyone who so wished could exercise the profession of goldsmith, without any limitations and in the most absolute freedom, since a period of apprenticeship with the obligatory presentation of a masterpiece for judgement was no

longer considered necessary. This new situation certainly presented the risk of improvisations and abuses, but the state of great competition and the high levels of quality demanded by buyers led to the rapid isolation of last-minute or poorly prepared artisans. Although its creation was not overseen by guilds, the silver produced during the Empire period is only rarely of mediocre quality; instead, in some cases it achieves noticeable improvements in comparison with certain late 18th-century pieces. In most cases the metal used is thick and robust, most of all in the moulded areas, which are far more solid than laminated or hammered silver. This solidity contributes to conferring a rigid and austere appearance on some objects, an appearance that is only heightened by the Empire style's regularity of forms and decoration, an aspect of the style with which some people find fault. The opening of the craft to new members and the suppression of the guilds also brought in new ideas, some of them previously unknown to the working of silver, and led in some cases to the introduction of innovative tech-

Rundell, Bridge & Rundell

Philip Rundell, born in 1743 in Widcombe, near Bristol, moved to London and joined the workshop of William Pickett, located in Ludgate Hill; he became a partner in 1777 and in 1785 took over the shop. He was described as an extremely eccentric man, ill-tempered but gifted with rare imagination and undisputed technical skills. In 1788 he made John Bridge his partner and in 1803 added his cousin Edmund Rundell to the association. Rundell, Bridge & Rundell were purveyors to the crown until 1839. Their works were so enormously successful with the English aristocracy and upper society that by 1806 their facto-ries employed more than a thousand workers. The firm made use of leading designers and skilled silversmiths. Much use was made of the neoclassical designs of the sculptors John Flaxman and William Theed and the painter Thomas Stothard. In 1807 Paul Storr was made artistic director of Rundell, Bridge & Rundell (he remained an associate until 1819), and the company enjoyed contributions from other skilled silversmiths, including Digby Scott and Benjamin Smith.

EMPIRE DECORATIVE MOTIFS

The decorative motifs of the Empire period, cast and chased or, more rarely, engraved, can be divided in two categories: figures of people or animals and ornaments inspired by the plant world. The first appear primarily on important pieces of display plate and were inspired by allegorical or mythological models or those taken from classical antiquity and are characterized by marked stateliness and equilibrium and the elegance of the poses. The most common plant motifs are palmettes, laurel crowns, stylized garlands and acanthus leaves. The stylization of motifs was more pronounced than in the past, and the designs became particularly rigorous, with clear and regular outlines.

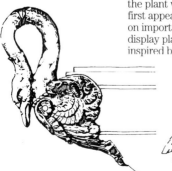

121

niques and original shapes and types. Such experiments would not have been possible under the strict control of guilds firmly anchored to the techniques and designs of the *ancien régime*. Striking examples of this new situation are provided by the bronzeworker Pierre-Philippe

Thomire and, even more, the cabinetmaker Martin Guillaume Biennais, both of whom became noted silversmiths.

New neoclassical forms

The Empire style is most easily understood when it is seen to present two equally convincing and valid aspects: on the one hand it was the last courtly style, and on the other it was the first middle-class style. At one and the same time, the style had to satisfy the demands of the new emerging middle class as well as those of its imperial sponsors, dedicated to imbuing every artistic work with a shining sense of its own

Puerperal cups

Puerperal cups came into being relatively recently: in fact the earliest examples date from the mid 18th century. Used primarily in Mediterranean countries, these are actually small tureens, usually shaped like a cup resting on a domed base with a cover and two handles, that were used for sipping hot broth.
Considered a source of quick energy, broth was often served to newly delivered mothers in need of strength after giving birth in order to ensure a healthy milk supply to feed their infants. These cups, which reached their greatest popularity in the period between the 18th and 19th centuries, were often part of a set that included a plate, fork and spoon, all held in an elegantly finished case. Such items were quite popular in Italy and were widespread in Milan; the head of the family would give his wife the set to mark the birth of the first male heir, and it would then become a symbol of the continuity of the family.

Opposite above: Puerperal cup in vermeil by Jean C. Cahier, Paris, 1797-1809. This is the classic model with opposed scroll handles.

Opposite below: Puerperal cup in vermeil, Paris, 1809-19. The cup is part of a set, including plate, fork and spoon, with a case.

Below left: Coffeepot in gilt silver in the shape of an elongated vase resting on three scrolled feet. By Martin Guillaume Biennais, Paris, 1809-19.

Below right: Empire coffeepot in gilt silver by Jean Baptiste Claude Odiot, Paris, 1809-19. Allegorical figures are applied to the smooth sides of the egg-shaped body.

greatness. And what forms could exalt power and glorious feats better than the neoclassical ones? Pieces of display plate in particular were created by adapting functional requirements to models gleaned from Greek, Etruscan and Roman remains. The types of silver made during this period repeat those already known

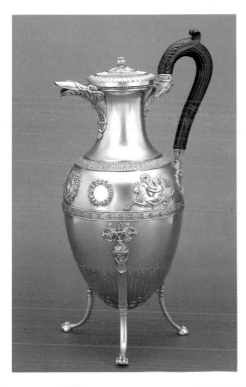

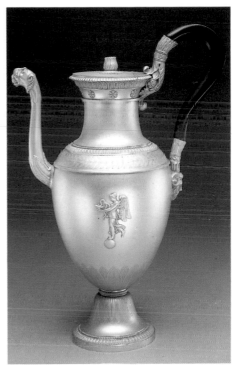

HALLMARKS OF FRENCH SILVERSMITHS

The hallmarks of French silversmiths of the Empire period are composed of a diamond shield with the smith's initials accompanied by a distinctive symbol, known as the *différent*. This type of hallmark had already been in use during the period of the revolution, when it was always presented vertically. From 1797 the masters used both horizontal and vertical arrangements.

Martin-Guillaume Biennais

Abel-Étienne Giroux

Marc-Augustin Lebrun

Antoine Boullier

Jean-Charles Cahier

Marie-Joseph-Gabriel Genu

Jacques-Frédéric Kirstein

Pierre Paraud

François-Dominique Naudin

Henry Auguste

Jean-Baptiste-Claude Odiot

François Daniel Imlin

123

and used at the end of the previous century; the only new introductions were the samovar and a particular type of round covered sugar bowl encircled by a support for twelve coffee spoons. The substantial differences thus involved ornamental appearances. Artisans no longer worked out the designs for their creations but instead drew abundantly from the collections of models of decorators, and in particular from those prepared by the government architects Percier and Fontaine. Their designs are marked by a strong architectural sense, perceptible in the structure and bal-

ance of the compositions, and by their respect for geometry and symmetry. The great formal pieces of silver such as terrines, salt and sugar containers, tureens, or vegetable dishes, often stand on monumental bases, in many cases further reinforced by the notable presence of sculptural components.

During the period of the Consulate and in the early years of the Empire these austere, elegant forms triumphed, but they became progressively heavier, almost as if seeking to reaffirm, against all evidence, the declining power of the regime.

The decorative repertory of the Empire style

One of the elements that most contributes to making Empire silver so recognizable is its decoration. The purely decorative aspect of a piece is never part of the object's formal definition, but, particularly during the early years, it is presented with sufficient discretion as not to even minimally disturb the piece's sculptural value. Silversmiths, like other French artisans of this period, drew on the official repertory, the themes of which can be divided into two large categories: those figurative and those inspired by plant motifs. Animal subjects, human figures, classical scenes and allegorical figures appear principally on the important pieces of display plate made for imperial or aristocratic patrons. On many pieces, the bas-relief elements applied to smooth, shiny bodies present allegorical scenes that pay homage to the glory of the state, to

Opposite above:
Coffeepot by Gaetano
Pane, Naples, 1807-30.
The masks attaching
the feet are in the
shape of medallions
of female busts.

Opposite bottom:
Coffeepot by Carlo
Bortolotti, Rome,
1790-1810. Also shown
is a detail of the
Medusa mask
beneath the spout.

Below: Large coffeepot
in silver made in
Catania in 1813.
The somewhat stocky
bellied body stands
on three classic feet.

"Fondu ciselé"

During the Napoleonic period a new method of working silver, known as fondu ciselé, *spread through France. This process, borrowed from bronze working, involves separately casting and then chasing different elements of the same object, such as, for example, the knop of a lid (which may itself be in several sections), the handles, the feet, or even decorative elements, such as friezes, bas-reliefs, and medallions. These different elements are then put together using either solder, the traditional method, or cleverly disguised screws and nuts. This latter technique of assembly, called* monture à froid *("cold mounting"), already being used at the end of Louis XIV's reign, became very common during the Empire period, when it was practiced with exceptional skill and precision. Henri Auguste (1759-1816) was the first of many to exploit this technique, but he was later joined by Jean Baptiste Claude Odiot (1763-1850), who cooperated with Thomire, a bronze-worker skilled in this type of work, to create a toilet service for the Empress Marie-Louise. The technique, which was both easier and quicker than embossing, also marked the beginning of the industrial manufacture of silver objects, since it allowed for the repetition of identical elements on different pieces, thus facilitating the process of mass production. Some scholars hold that this brought an end to unique works in the traditional sense.*

Justice, or to Plenty, or represent the nations of Europe humbled. Equally frequent are subjects of mythological inspiration or those drawn from antiquity, such as sphinxes, winged horses and lions, sea horses, eagles, swans, or entwined serpents that form handles.

All these motifs are characterized by a marked stateliness with static and elegant poses. Plant elements were originally used as frames for these figural representations or as the sole decorations only for less important pieces. Such elements later appear in the decorative repertories with greater regularity, although any naturalistic accents declined in favour of increased stylization. The designs became more rigorous, with strongly marked and regular outlines and

EMPIRE

Below: Teapot in silver by Stephen Adam, London, 1806-7. The classic, squarish shape is typical of English silvers of this period.

Bottom: Handled cup made in Russia dating from the period 1782-1808. The decorations display close affinities to classic Empire motifs.

ancient Egyptians, which was taken up, reinterpreted, and used by various artists and obtained much general approval. The most common motifs in what came to be called the Egyptian style are sphinxes, stylized lotus flowers, ovolos, palmettes and symbolic figures taken from Egyptian statuary, such as the sun god Horus, represented by a central disk from which spread two wings.

French silversmiths

The technical skills of many artisans made important contributions to the great success that French Empire silver enjoyed both at home and abroad. Among these many artisans the names of three stand out: Auguste, Odiot and Biennais. Henri Auguste (1759-1816), son of a silversmith, perpetuated typically 18th-century elegance in works distinguished by architectural forms with light, highly

reliefs; symmetry dominates, the proportions are impeccable, the rhythms precise. The idealization of concept was matched by powerful creative imagination. Palmettes are one of the most common themes, but they appear together with an infinity of other motifs: laurel crowns, garlands of stylized leaves, horns of plenty, rosettes and acanthus and thyrse leaves.

The "retour d'Egypte"

A singular characteristic of the Empire style's decorative repertory is referred to by the French as the "*retour d'Egypte*." Admiral Horatio Nelson's defeat of the French fleet on August

1, 1798, off Abukir (the battle of the Nile), ended the ill-fated Egyptian campaign, and Napoleon, as general of the French army, returned to Paris with many archaeological finds that awakened great interest in many artists, artisans and scholars. Napoleon himself, fascinated by the artistic wealth of the land of the pyramids, decided to send an expedition to study and catalogue the treasures. The result of this was reported by Vivant Denon in his *Travels in Upper and Lower Egypt*, published in Paris in 1802 and translated into English in 1803. This book contributed further to the popularity of the ornamentation used by the

refined decoration. When he was made bankrupt in 1806 and forced into exile, his models were acquired by Jean-Baptiste-Claude Odiot (1763-1850), another member of a dynasty of silversmiths. He was inspired by the designs of Percier and Fontaine as well as by those of Prud'hon and Cavelier, and his fame spread beyond France's borders, earning him a vast clientele in foreign countries.

Martin Guillaume Biennais (1764-1843), Napoleon's official silversmith, stands apart as probably the best artist at interpreting the Empire style, and his works are distinguished not just by the variety of types he made but also by the way he perfectly matched form to decoration. Together with these three masters, more than three hundred silversmiths were active in the city of Paris alone; among them were fine artisans, many of whom were trained in shops run by Biennais and Odiot, such as Jean-Charles Cahier, Marie-Joseph-Gabriel Genu, Abel-Etienne Giroux, and Lorillon, Naudin, Fauconnier and Paraud. The centralization brought about under Napoleon led to the leading artists being concentrated in Paris, where studios were quickly set up, some of them of considerable size. The provinces lost some of the aspects that had made their fortune during the 18th century. Many artisans there went into commerce selling objects from Parisian workshops and thus capable of satisfying a great volume of requests; others in effect worked on commission for goldsmiths in the capital.

Even so, some centers maintained a high level of prestige, and the cites on the nation's borders contributed to the diffusion of Empire silver abroad. Strasbourg, in particular, thanks to the works of Kirstein and Imlin, carried on the tradition of vermeil for which the city was famous.

The influence of Empire silver outside France

The Empire style exercised considerable influence on many European countries. The diffusion of French taste throughout Europe was largely a result of Napoleon's expansionistic aims, which

EMPIRE

provided for on 18 Brumaire of the year VI (November 9, 1797). Napoleon's policies thus had a direct effect on the Empire style's fortune in Europe, but an equally preponderant role was played by the leading silversmiths of Paris, who exported masterpieces to many European capitals in response to commissions from royal and aristocratic patrons. Many of these works have survived and are today preserved in important museums. The leader in this was Odiot, who with the assistance of skilled associates served the principal courts of Europe for a good dozen years. An outstanding example of these works is the table service probably made for Maria Fedorovna (believed by some scholars to have been ordered by her son, Michel Pavlovitch, in 1809), parts of which are now preserved in the

brought France to the direct or indirect political control of a good part of the continent. Particularly in those countries connected to the French empire, the weight of French rule involved not just the social, political and administrative aspects of life but also those tied to cultural and artistic affairs, for Napoleon considered these an ideal vehicle for propaganda exalting his own magnificence. In the field of silver, aside from the dominance of Parisian models on style, this control extended to how silver was made and sold, with the creation of new departments and with the establishment of a hallmark (and guarantees of purity), as had been

THE "EGYPTIAN" STYLE IN GREAT BRITAIN

The enthusiastic response to Horatio Nelson's victory over the French fleet at Abukir (1798) awakened a great interest in the so-called Egyptian style in England. Although not numerous, several pieces of English silver were decorated with sphinxes, ovolos, palmettes and stylized lotus flowers, clearly based on Egyptian statuary.

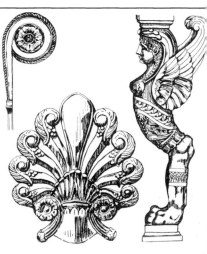

Left: Centerpiece com-
posed of a cylindrical
base mounted with a
column flanked by
winged sphinxes. By
Martin Guillaume
Biennais, Paris, 1797-
1809.

Bottom: Oval tureen
with pedestal base; the
ring on the cover is
formed by a coiling
snake. By Paul Storr,
London, 1808.

The majesty of these objects
along with the diffusion of
models made by the most
celebrated designers, had an
enormous influence on the
work of European silver-
smiths, although artisans
outside France rarely succeeded in creating objects of
a stylistic purity equal to
those of France. Many of the
pieces produced display
regional styles mixed with
Empire motifs, which are
most often poorly interpreted and are simply trans-
posed in a tired and repetitive manner.

Hermitage, parts in the
Rijksmuseum, and parts in
the Espirito Santo foundation of Lisbon. No less
important is the toilet service made for Marie-Louise
of Austria in collaboration
with the bronze-worker
Thomire based on designs
by Prud'hon; the original
was destroyed by the
empress herself, but the
designs remain as witness
to the work's grandiosity.

England in the early 19th century

More than any other
European country, Great
Britain remained immune to
the political and cultural
hegemony of Napoleon. In
constant conflict with the
French empire, having suffered grave governmental
and economic crises at the

Martin Guillaume Biennais

Together with Henri Auguste
and Jean Baptiste Claude
Odiot, Martin Guillaume
Biennais (1764-1843) is considered one of the leading
interpreters of French silver
in the Empire period. He
opened a shop in 1789 as a
cabinetmaker under the sign
of a violet monkey (which
shows up in his hallmark)
and changed to silverworking
following the revolutionary
laws of 1791 and 1797 that
abolished guilds, permitting
anyone to exercise the trade
without apprenticeship and
without presenting a masterpiece for review. He became
Napoleon's favourite silversmith (partly, it was said,
because he had extended him
credit during the period of the
Egyptian campaign); among
the works commissioned by
the emperor was a tea service
with Sèvres porcelain cups
today in the Louvre. Awarded
a gold medal at the Exposition
des Produits de l'Industrie in
1806, his fame grew enor-
mously, and he received commissions from the courts of all
Europe, in particular those of
Austria, Bavaria and Russia.
In addition, his middle-class
clientele grew steadily, and he
is thought to have employed
no fewer than six hundred
workers and numbered
among his collaborators
such skilled silversmiths as
Cahièr, Genu, Giroux,
Lorillon and Naudin. Often
using models by the celebrated decorator Percier (models
attributed to Percier were
found in the an album belonging to Biennais), he created a
great variety of silver objects
in the Empire style distinguished by refined balance.

beginning of the century, and deprived of commercial supremacy on the Continent, Britain nevertheless maintained its independence, as is made abundantly clear by various artistic expressions. Not that there were no contacts between English culture and developments across the Channel: many models by Auguste were appreciated and copied, several French artisans fled to London, and even Odiot himself worked alongside Garrard by the Thames. But perhaps out of hostility for France and for the style that embodied Napoleonic glory, the English artisans worked in their own language, even though this was not always coherent or recognizable from homogeneous characteristics.

From the stylistic point of view, this period is called Regency, although the term is somewhat imprecise and inadequate. In historical terms, Regency refers to the last nine years (1811-20) of the reign of George III, when the king's insanity had rendered him unfit to rule and the government was vested in the prince of Wales (later George IV); in the history of decorative arts, Regency is applied to the period that runs from the end of the 18th century to 1830, the year of George IV's death. It thus indicates the period of transition from the rigorous, almost

academic neoclassicism imposed by Adam to the fierce eclecticism that marked the Victorian period, the first clear signs of which were then just beginning to appear.

English silver between neoclassicism and eclecticism

Early on, the Regency style freed itself from the stylistic preoccupations inspired

Opposite top: Coupe de mariage *with allegorical motifs. The handles are shaped like cornucopias, and the finial is a female figure holding a ewer and basin. By Odiot, Paris, 1797-1809.*

Opposite bottom: Tureen in gilt silver by Martin Guillaume Biennais, Paris, 1797-1809. The smooth vase-shaped body rests on a round base standing on six feet.

Bottom: Tureen with smooth oval body with tiny beading along the border. The finial is a swan with folded wings. By Antoine Boullier, Paris, 1797-1809.

The Odiots

The craft of silversmith is one of those artisan trades traditionally handed down from father to son, and the Odiot family stands out in the general panorama of French "dynasties" of master silversmiths. The founder of the family business was Jean Baptiste Gaspard (made master in 1720, he died in 1777); but it was with Jean Baptiste Claude (born in 1763, made master in 1785, and died in 1850) that the Odiots reached the highest peaks with the neoclassical and Empire styles. The patronage of Napoleon's family permitted the production of silver of truly extraordinary magnificence and technical artistry. After the fall of Napoleon, the crowned heads of Europe continued to commission works. The family's continuity was assured by Charles Nicolas, who had worked with his father during his father's period of maturity and thus made accurate reproductions of the family models. With Jean Baptiste Gustave (1823-1912), the family's tradition for great silver remained unchanged, still characterized by technical artistry and large-scale production. Because models were handed down within the Odiot family "company," the hallmarks on any given piece must be carefully examined to determine which of the masters made it.

by the work of Adam and elaborated a synthesis of forms and decoration that ranged freely from notions taken from Egyptian ornaments to those that were typically rococo. Much of the silver produced was influenced by designs made by the sculptors John Flaxman and William Theed as well as the painter Thomas Stothard, who were more interested in informing their pieces with an effect of grandeur and solidity, often obtained using sculptural ornamentation, than in attempting any aesthetical-theoretical justifications for the use of differing decorative elements.

The appeal of classical antiquity is one of the keys to understanding the new creations of this period; figures in full relief, such as caryatids, sphinxes, or alle-

gorical scenes came back into fashion, and in some cases artisans went so far as to make faithful reproductions of archaeological finds, in particular Roman terracottas. At the same time and parallel to this tendency was a rediscovery of exoticism, of the Gothic and most of all the rococo, in which the entire decorative repertory was dusted off and repro posed, although in a somewhat tired and heavy manner; thus scrolling leaves, fringed seashells, flowers and masks return to decorate every type of object, often combined in an eclectic way with various neoclassical elements.

Silversmiths

The economic difficulties England experienced at the beginning of the centu-

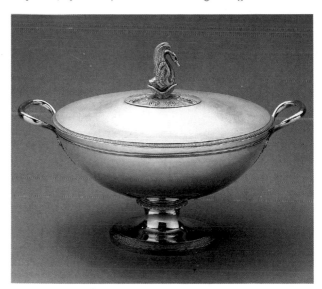

Below: Tureen made by
Paul Storr, London,
1802-3. The fluted rib-
bon handles are
attached to the body
with relief masks of
lions' heads.

Bottom: Large center-
piece in the Egyptian
style, resting on a trian-
gular base that stands
on three animal-paw
feet. Paul Storr,
London, 1820.

Opposite bottom:
Tureen made in
Messina early in the
19th century.
The finial is a
sculptural figure of
a crouching lion.

ry had only slight effects on the production of silver, which remained quantitatively high. The number of artisans employed in the trade was reasonably large, although their work was beginning to be threatened by the first applications of industrial processes, the products of which were still of low quality but also lower prices.

The most important new aspect of the silver trade was the appearance of a new role. Until this period artisans would make and sell their own works and deal directly with customers, but the growth of production, enlargement of the market across increasingly broad social levels, and growth in size of many of the workshops led to the appearance of the tradesman.

The precursor of this new way of making and selling silver, halfway between the artisan workshop and the modern company, was without doubt Philip Rundell, planner and founder of what became the celebrated firm of Rundell, Bridge & Rundell, holder of the royal warrant for jewellery and goldsmith's work; indeed, the king himself spent exorbitant sums on their work. Rundell displayed his business acumen in what were for that period decidedly original notions, and as early as 1806 the firm had more

Left: One of a pair
of tureens with cover
by John Houle, London,
1816-19. The feet are
joined to the body
with scrolled foliate
masks.

Paul Storr

*Paul Storr (1771-1844) is
without doubt the most
famous English silversmith of
the Regency period. He was
apprenticed to Andrew
Fogelburg in 1785, entered a
partnership with William
Frisbee in 1792, registered his
own mark in London in
January 1793, and opened a
shop at 20 Ayr Street,
Piccadilly. In 1807 he moved
to Dean Street, Soho, and
from then until 1819 he
worked with the prestigious
firm of Rundell, Bridge &
Rundell, purveyors to King
George III. In 1822 he formed
a partnership with John
Mortimer, Storr & Mortimer,
which lasted until Storr's
retirement in 1838. Collectors
are particularly fond of his
neoclassical works, especially
the pieces of display plate
produced in great number
on commission for the Prince
of Wales and his court. His
works, sometimes confused
with those of his students
Benjamin Smith and Digby
Scott, are distinguished by
solid bodies of impressive size
that are often gilt. His works
are always of excellent quality, but those he made
between 1800 and 1825 (the
period of his association with
Rundells), which are characterized by the use of typical
decorative elements (handles
with lion's heads, foliate feet,
etc.) and elegant propor-
tions, are generally preferred
to his early work, which
shows the influence of
Fogelburg.*

than a thousand employees
and made much use of the
collaboration of designers
from other disciplines,
such as the sculptors Flaxman and Theed and the
painter Stothard.

Furthermore, the London
firm made use of the work
of the best artisans of the
period, such as Digby Scott,
Benjamin Smith and, most
of all, Paul Storr. Without

doubt the best-known silversmith of the period, Storr
was particularly distin
guished for his monumental
works, such as large table
services and display plate.
Often based on designs
made by Flaxman, Storr's
work originally displayed
many neoclassical features,
but it soon evolved towards
the neorococo that Storr
himself helped to form.

PS

Vinaigrettes

An outgrowth of the pomander, or spice box, vinaigrettes are small boxes with a hinged cover made to hold a sponge soaked in aromatic vinegars. This was held in place by a small grille that was itself attached by a hinge to the base. Gilded on the inside to prevent corrosion and used both to combat unpleasant odours and to cure fainting fits, vinaigrettes were made in large numbers between 1800 and 1840, although some examples date from the last twenty years of the 18th century, and a considerable number were made right up to 1900. Most vinaigrettes are rectangular, but many were made in the most varied of forms: suitcases, barrels, nuts, fish, books, hearts, seashells, flowers, beehives and so on. Some were decorated with semiprecious stones, others are engraved with ornamental motifs or landscape or architectural scenes. The grille that held the sponge a simple pierced plaque or may be a piece of intricate filigree work.

Presentation silver

The types of silver made during these years were those that had been established at the end of the 18th century. Certain traditional forms, characteristic of English silver production, were perpetuated by adjusting them to different stylistic requirements.

One new silver type did appear during this period: so-called presentation silver, pieces designed and made specifically as gifts. Of course, silver had always been considered particularly suitable for presentation on special occasions, ceremonies or anniversaries, in large part because of the metal's obvious precious character. Until this period, gifts had been chosen from among the usual types of silver in use, but in the Regency period presentation silver became widespread in a series of objects made to be given as gifts and thus, aside from any practical function, made in response to certain symbolic needs, usually related to a particular occasion or ceremony. The celebratory nature of many of these objects is most often emphasized by a

*Below: One of a pair of
wine coolers with an
upturned-bell body
standing on a pedestal
base. Hennel & Terrey,
London, 1814.*

*Bottom: Cup and cover
made by Benjamin
Smith for Rundell,
Bridge & Rundell in
1807. It is based on the
celebrated "Trafalgar
Cup" today preserved in
the Victoria and Albert
Museum, London.*

highest expression and can be taken as characteristic of much of the flatware made in the 19th century. In some cases, particularly in France, handles or even entire pieces were gilded to give greater importance to services already made impressive by austere decorations of classical inspiration. This period also saw great technological progress that led to the first mass production of forged-iron blades.

The propensity for inventing new elements to complete table services continued, and services were enriched by utensils matched to particular dinner courses: for appetizers, for

noble, monumental appearance, as is the case with the famous Trafalgar Cups that were made in 1805-56 by Scott and Smith to designs by Flaxman and were offered by the Lloyds Patriotic Fund to distinguished officers who had participated in the famous battle.

Flatware during the first years of the 19th century

No further evolution took place in the shapes and types of flatware during the first years of the 19th century; the knife, fork and spoon had already assumed precise and nearly definitive forms during the 18th century.

Several special characteristics of Empire flatware, however, are worthy of mention. During this period, the tendency to reproduce and make larger and larger flatware, a movement that had appeared at the end of the 18th century, reached its

REGENCY

One of a pair of vegetable dishes by Jorgen Buch, St. Petersburg, 1802. The circular body has chased borders, and the cover has a variety of decorations. The finial is shaped like a fruit on a foliate base.

fish, for salad, for desserts. The most common patterns during this period were still those inherited from the 18th-century tradition, although they were presented in infinite varieties; the only pattern that, although already known, came to enjoy great popularity dur-

ing these years, first in Great Britain and then in the rest of Europe, was the so-called King's pattern, a violin-shaped handle decorated with shells framed by a border running the entire length of the handle. The knife maintained its long, straight blade with rounded

or pointed end, and the handle, also straight, was decorated in various ways. Several interesting variations of classical designs appeared, particularly in France, including handles with sheaved motifs and others in rectangular section with straight sides tapering towards the blade setting.

A distinctive characteristic of Empire flatware is the presence of ornamental motifs running the entire length of the handle rather than being concentrated only on the spatula of forks and spoons or on the ends of knife handles, as had been common in preceding periods. The decoration is based on the ornamental motifs of the period blended with motifs from classical antiquity: palmettes, lyres, garlands of flowers, acanthus leaves, seashells and allegorical figures, in most cases set within and framed by simple linear decoration.

Several 19th-century Russian hallmarks

SAINT PETERSBURG		MOSCOW		NOVOGOROD	RIGA	ODESSA	
1815	1801	1777-1861	1867-71 (1870)	1851-62	19th cent.	1843	1848

KIEV		VLADIMIR	TULA		ASTRAKHAN	KALUGA	SMOLENSK
1828-87	1892-96	1857-63 (1857)	1796-1838	1874	1828	between 18th and 19th cent.	1844-45

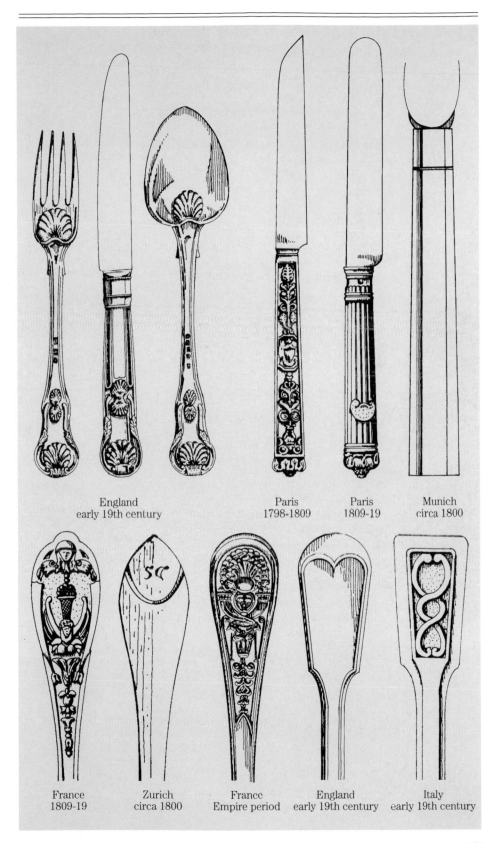

England
early 19th century

Paris
1798-1809

Paris
1809-19

Munich
circa 1800

France
1809-19

Zurich
circa 1800

France
Empire period

England
early 19th century

Italy
early 19th century

SEVERAL 19TH-CENTURY HALLMARKS

Italy

ROME

from 1815   1870-72

VENICE

1805   early 19th cent.

1810-15

TRIESTE

1806   1805   1805   1806-7

MILAN

from 1810

MODENA

1810-72

PARMA

1818-72

LUCCA

1801-10   1810-47

1848-72

GENOA

from 1824

TURIN

1814-24   from 1824

KINGDOM OF SARDINIA

1825-72   1824-72

France

		1798-1809	1809-19	1819-38
Assay mark	Paris			
	Department			
Silver standard	Paris		Grosse garantie	Grosse garantie
	Department		Moyenne garantie	Moyenne garantie

Portugal

LISBON

early 19th cent.   1816-28   1881-86

OPORTO

1810-18   1843-53   1853-62   1870-77

BRAGA

1800-30

ÉVORA

18th-19th cent.

GUIMARÃES

19th cent.

SETÚBAL

early 19th cent.

Low Countries

AMSTERDAM   ROTTERDAM   ZWOLLE   LEIDEN

1800-14

BELGIUM

1814-31   1831-68

Scandinavian Countries

BERGEN

1815   1856

COPENHAGEN

1801   1827   1850

AALBORG

19th cent.

AARHUS

19th cent.

VIBORG

19th cent.

HELSINKI

1810-1943

KUOPIO

1810-1943

TAMPERE

1810-1943

ARBOGA

19th cent.

GÖTEBORG

19th cent.

FALUN

19th cent.

LULEÅ

19th cent.

UPPSALA

19th cent.

YSTAD

19th cent.

NORRKÖPING

19th cent.

RESTORATION

The new European situation

After the downfall of the Napoleonic empire, Europe was completely redesigned by the Congress of Vienna (1814-15). Napoleon's dream of European hegemony vanished, leaving room for quite different views that primarily sought the restoration of the pre-revolutionary dynastic and territorial states. The political, social and economic situation that these restored crowned heads had to confront was in great contrast to what they had left behind. The years of French domination and the long wars had swept away much of the structure of Europe and had profound effects on the productive resources of the individual states, and the social upheavals following the French Revolution had left an indelible mark: the middle class had grown stronger, and although political power was still beyond its grasp, it already controlled economic power. The restored monarchies revealed themselves to be weak and vulnerable, undermined by the emerging class and denied the social prestige and material wealth that had supported them in the 18th century. Inevitably, this new situation had an effect on the development of the decorative arts, and silver in particular. With the abolition of 18th-century-style guilds and with the almost total withdrawal of the court from matters related to art, the artisans found themselves suddenly without the points of reference that had guided their work throughout the 18th century and, at least for a short time, they proved incapable of furnishing any precise or coherent style to their clientele. For their part, the potential buyers were becoming increasingly heterogeneous and interested primarily in reasonably-priced pieces, made possible by the increased use of machines.

Opposite top: Salver in gilt silver by Benjamin Smith, London, 1823. The border of this circular salver is decorated with shells, masks and flowers; a coat of arms is engraved at the center.

Opposite bottom: Sugar bowl in gilt silver by Charles Nicolas Odiot, Paris, mid 19th century. Two sculptural figures flank the vase-shaped container and stand on an oval base with four feet.

Below: Pair of handled trays by Philip Rundell, London, 1823. The trays stand on eight feet and are finely engraved with framed coats of arms.

Persistence and decline of the Empire style

The Empire style, which had appeared before Napoleon took power, survived his fall by several years. There are various reasons for this stylistic persistence, but perhaps the most revealing was the inability of the new monarchies to impose their own style. As a result, the existing style, widespread and solidly rooted in many European courts, was able to hold its own, purged only of the most obvious Napoleonic symbols. Thus Louis XVIII of France was able to instal himself in the imperial apartments without making any changes to their style.

Many of the silversmiths who had distinguished themselves in the Empire period, such as Odiot and Cahier, carried on their tradition, continuing to serve various European courts even during the years of the Restoration. Empire silver thus survived another decade, but it progressively lost many of its essential characteristics. Among the various circumstances that caused its eventual decline were the great financial and economic difficulties troubling many nations, which imposed a style of life on

141

Right: Inkstand by Saverio Caletti, Milan, 1820-28. The rectangular tray has a grillwork border and bears two urn-shaped containers and a central penholder.

all social levels that was very different from imperial pomp. Nostalgia for the *ancien régime* slowly led to a revival of past styles; competition with industrial production began to have a considerable impact; and the influence of English silversmiths spread on the Continent. The pure and elegant

forms that had characterized the early years of the century slowly grew heavier, and the broad smooth

surfaces slowly became covered with abundant decoration, complex and oppressive, that abandoned the original rigour. Compact and tiresome floral motifs appeared with increasing persistence on silver; the motif of the stylized palmette, so common throughout the Napoleonic period, gave place to compound associations of acanthus leaves that often overflow their borders to invade other areas of the piece. These were the first symptoms of the artistic tendencies that reached their full expression in the eclectic period.

THEMES AND DECORATIVE MOTIFS IN THE RESTORATION PERIOD

Unlike the other decorative arts, silver did not develop an independent or original language during the Restoration period, but rather presented many of the themes that had characterized the Empire period. These, however, slowly lost many of their principal qualities as adaptations were made to serve the needs of the new middle class, who requested a more subdued, less luxurious or

showy elegance. At first rigorous and austere, the decoration

became softer, more complicated, heavier, giving life to overloading that sometimes became excessive. Motifs of classical inspiration, such as dolphins, swans, lyres and crowns, were made softer using rounded profiles and less symmetrical layouts, elements of plant inspiration appeared with increasing frequency along with gadrooning and sculptural elements, and embossing and chasing enjoyed a rediscovery.

Opposite below:
Inkstand by Angelo
Giannotti, Rome, first
half 19th century. The
oval tray with pierced
border bears amphora-
shaped containers with
covers finished with
sculptural elements.

Below: Cruet stand
by Gaetano Boschetti,
Milan, c. 1840.
The rectangular tray
supports a vertical han-
dle to which are fixed
rings to hold
the bottles.

Bottom left: Coffeepot
from Genoa dating
from 1824-72. The ovoid
body stands on three
long feet that end in
animal paws, and the
spout ends in an ani-
mal head.

Bottom right: Coffeepot
by Emanuele Caber,
Milan, c. 1830. The
amphora-shaped body,
base and spout are
enlivened by ribbing,
and the spout is shaped
like an animal head.

The influence of English silver

The fall of the French empire was followed by reciprocal exchanges of artistic styles among the countries of Europe. In terms of silver English taste and tradition, as interpreted in the Regency period, spread to many areas of continental Europe. For historical reasons, some European states had remained tied to Anglo-Saxon culture even during the Napoleonic domination, but others discovered only now the shapes and decorations in vogue on the other side of the Channel. For example, during the early years of the 19th century the silver made in Scandinavian countries is in a neoclassical style nearer the dictates of Adam than those of contemporary designers in France. In France itself, homeland of the Empire style, English taste had, for obvious political reasons, not enjoyed much favour, but it now took hold, particularly during the reign of Charles X (1824-30). Among the reasons for this is the fact that the many French artisans who had fled to the British Isles during the revolution returned with the restoration of the monarchy, bringing with them the ideas and stylistic traits they had assimilated during their years in Britain. These cultural exchanges were fur-

Below: One of a pair of candelabra by Paul Storr, London, 1834-35. The base is richly embossed with rococo motifs, and the stem has vertical fluting of plant elements.

Below right: Coffeepot with warmer by John Bridge, London, 1831-32. The tapering cylindrical body is enlivened by rounded vertical fluting, as are the base and cover.

Opposite bottom: Teapot with warmer by Fabergé, Moscow, 1890. The polylobate body with alternating foliate elements and cartouches rests on a tripod with lion's-paw feet.

ther strengthened by travels and collaborations among the leading artisans of the two countries (Odiot worked in London for Garrard, Vechte worked for Storr, Mortimer & Hunt), which spread to France the simple forms of English tradition (smooth, rounded teapots, oval coffeepots and so on) along with certain decorative themes then in vogue, most of all motifs of plant inspiration and a certain type of gadrooning, using alternating larger and smaller lobes arranged vertically or at angles, that was used to finish the borders of plates and salvers.

Various production areas in Italy were affected by the influence of English style, primarily as a result of commercial contacts between English cities and the major port cities of the peninsula. For example, the many artisans active in Genoa often produced pieces characterized by a close stylistic affinity with the sober and elegant neoclassical production based on models by Adam.

Much the same can be said of various works in silver of Sicilian manufacture, although in this case the reasons behind the English influence must be traced to quite different motivations. In fact, the inhabitants of Britain had discovered that Sicilian marsala wine made a fine alternative to Spanish sherry, and during their frequent trips to Sicily the members of the wine trade commissioned silver in the neoclassical style from silversmiths in Palermo, Messina and Catania. They regularly brought these pieces to England on their return trips.

European production

The grave economic situation in the countries of the Iberian peninsula effectively suspended the production of silver for civilian use, and religious objects offered the only outlet for local artisans. Among the only pieces worthy of note was the table triumph given to the duke of Wellington by don João in celebration of the victory at Waterloo. The work involved 142 artisans, including the sculptors Pines de Gama and João Texera Pinto, who worked on it for three years, from 1813 to 1816, under the direction of the painter

19th-century flatware

Over the course of the 19th century the types of flatware in use multiplied enormously with frequent, sometimes constant, resort made to models from the preceding century, which were continually re-interpreted and reworked in innumerable variations in terms of both shape and decoration. The decorative motifs, in particular, multi-

Antonio Domingos de Sequeira. Also worthy of note is the silver made in Holland; the northern Low Countries assimilated the stylistic dictates of the Empire style in only insignificant amounts and tended instead towards simple, essential forms, almost free of ornament. The decoration was limited to basic moulding or fluting that served to emphasize the bare lines and smooth surfaces of the pieces. Only after the fall of Napoleon were the German-language areas able to fully develop their own neoclassical style, and this was influenced in large part by the studies and works published by Johann Joachim Winckelmann (1717-68). Particularly after the publication in 1821 of a series of models for silver designed by the architect and painter Karl Friedrich Schinkel (1781-1841), the leading artisans (Hossauer, Stier, and Neuss among them) began making works free from any ties with the other artistic cultures of Europe. In France, there were the works of Charles Cahier and Fauconnier. Inspired by models by

Lafitte, they made a series of silver objects that demonstrate the recourse to sculptural elements, embossing and chasing that were to become constant traits of French silver in the years to come.

Below left: Cup and
cover made by John
Bridge for Rundell,
Bridge & Co., London,
1831. This is based on
Gothic models but
decorated in the
eclectic style.

Below: Centerpiece by
Benjamin Smith II,
London, 1823. The bas-
ket is supported by a
long fluted stem and by
three classical figures
with ancient musical
instruments.

plied in copious rework-
ings of types inherited
from the 18th-century tradition and with the
increasingly continuous
use of floral and plant
motifs (especially in the
period of the French
Second Republic) and
with the addition of ele-
ments marked by decora-
tive sculpture. The use of
moulds permitted the cre-
ation of pieces of the same
form and decoration for
their entire length, with

no break in continuity.
Handles were made in a
shape that spread out and
widened from the stem
without interruptions.
Knife handles were gener-
ally straight, with the end
rounded, although other
shapes chosen at random
from among past styles
were not rare. The blade
returned to having a usu-
ally rounded point, with
the spine and cutting edge
straight and parallel; in
the second half of the cen-

tury the blade grew shorter and took on a shape
similar to a spatula, making it easier to push food
on to the fork. In this type
the blade lost some of its
cutting ability, but this
was made up for with the
adoption of the first ser-
rated edges. With dining
flatware in particular
there was a return to the
use of handles of ebony or
ivory, often finely worked
or carved in imitation of
famous Renaissance mod-

Below: One of a pair of
sauceboats by Johann
Georg Christoph Neuss,
Augsburg, 1821. The
base is an oval pedestal
and the body bears
applied motifs of vines
and grapes.

Bottom: One of two wine
coolers in gilt silver by
the Barnards, London,
1836-37. The vase body
is richly embossed with
rocaille motifs and two
cartouches circumscrib-
ing a coat of arms.

els. The production of silver flatware was steady
and abundant, but there
was also growing experi-
mentation with new met-
als and new alloys, such as
iron, tin, brass, nickel and
nickel silver, materials
that were later plated.

These types became even
more popular with the perfection of the processes of
plating by electrolysis,
which permitted the mar-
keting of stylish services at
remarkably low prices that
made them accessible to a
vast range of buyers.

Wine coolers

*Wine coolers, also known as
ice pails, are items of domestic
silver made to chill a bottle by
immersing it in cold or iced
water. This type was made in
all the countries of Europe,
beginning around the last
thirty years of the 18th centu
ry, although examples exist
that date from the second
decade of the century. Wine
coolers are almost always two-
handled and of circular or
octagonal section. They were
usually made in pairs, each
to hold a single bottle (there
are, however, oval examples
large enough for two, such as
those in gilt silver made by
Digby Scott and Benjamin
Smith in 1805 and today in
the Royal Collection). Since
these were objects of display
plate, they are often richly
decorated in the style of the
period, although the form,
most of all during the neoclassical period, was generally
vase-shaped, even based on
the style of marble vases
found during archaeological
excavations. Examples of this
are the gilt-silver wine coolers
made in 1812 by Paul Storr
and known as Warwick vases,
reduced-size copies of a marble vase found in 1770 in
Hadrian's villa near Rome
(and then held at Warwick
Castle). Wine coolers were
made in numerous forms
and variations, however,
such as pails, barrels,
amphoras and basins. The
most important were made in
Great Britain, where many
were made by the leading silversmiths of the period.*

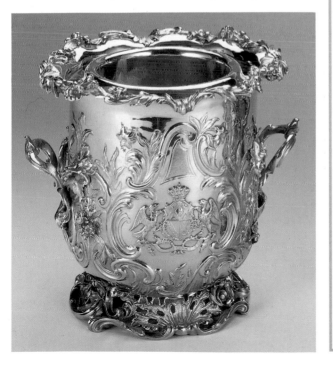

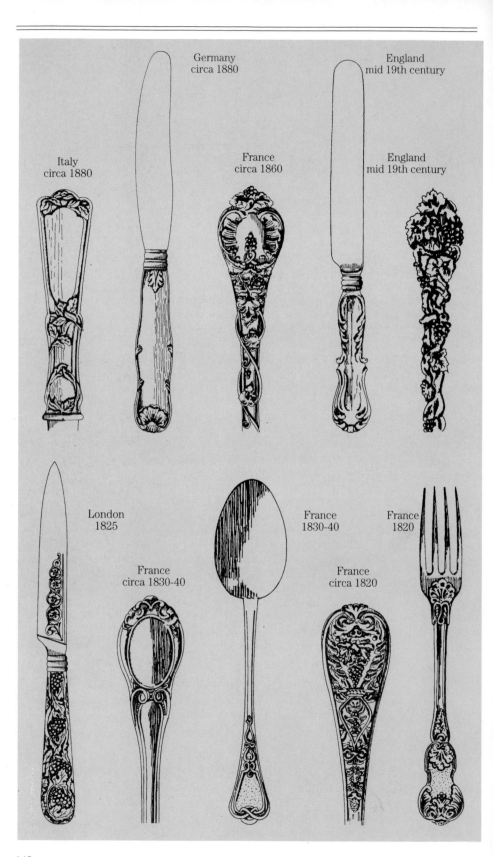

Italy
circa 1880

Germany
circa 1880

France
circa 1860

England
mid 19th century

England
mid 19th century

London
1825

France
circa 1830-40

France
1830-40

France
circa 1820

France
1820

SEVERAL 19TH-CENTURY HALLMARKS

German-language countries

ALTONA	BERLIN	BRESLAU	KASSEL	DARMSTADT	DESSAU
1850	19th cent.	1848	19th cent.	19th cent.	19th cent.

KARLSRUHE	DRESDEN	HAMBURG	NORDEN	HEILBRONN
from 1806	19th cent.	1800-1 1821	19th cent.	1846 19th cent.

KÖNIGSBERG	LUDWIGSBURG	LÜNEBURG	CONSTANCE	WÜRZBURG
1815 19th cent.	19th cent	early 19th cent.	19th cent.	early 19th cent.

NUREMBERG	PRUSSIA	WEIBURG	WISMAR	STUTTGART
early 19th cent.	1809 1809-12	18th-19th cent.	early 19th cent.	19th cent.

BUDAPEST	KRAKÓW	GRATZ
1800 1826 1859	1809-35 1835-66	1804 1806-7

PRAGUE	LINZ	KLAGENFURT	ÖDENBURG	PRESSBURG
1814-66	1806-7 1807-9	1801	1855	1843 1858

SALZBURG	VIENNA
1806 1806-7	1802 1806 1807 1806-7 1866 1872

ECLECTICISM

Below left: Large tankard and cover by Richard Hennel, London, 1872. An S-scroll handle and sculptural finial complete this richly decorated piece. Below right: One of a pair of pitchers in crystal with gilt-silver mounts, by C. Odiot, Paris, c. 1875. The mounts and cover are decorated with grape clusters and vine leaves. Bottom: Cup by Thomas, James and Nathaniel Creswick, London, 1851-52.

Silver at the height of the 19th century

Many of the trends that had already begun to characterize the production of silver following the fall of the French empire were further developed and affirmed during the years of the height of the 19th century. The return to earlier styles, increasing use of industrial methods, and heavy competition from "plated" objects are among the factors that most heavily influenced the production of silver during the eclectic period. The terms that are used to define the stylistic trends of this period or parts of it (eclecticism, historicism, romanticism and so on) reflect more a yearning for linguistic and conceptual simplification than any true ascertainment of an expressive cohesion, and as such they do not take into account the complexity of the situations, influences, and events that are at the base of this period. Rather than examine the distinctive traits taken in different geographical areas, an introduction to this period should emphasize the trends, important and pervasive, that are fundamental to any understanding of the evolution of the decorative arts in general and silver in particular. In the first place one must point out the important role played by the increasingly common "international exhibitions," singular occasions for discussion and comparison that crossed all national borders. Aside from affirming the increasing interest in industrialization and the attempts at rejuvenating artisan activities, these

Left: Salver in gilt silver by J. E. Terrey, London, 1844. The rim is embossed with allegorical scenes of pagan divinities. Bottom: Toilet mirror with silver frame, Vienna, 1840.

made among silversmiths and artisans or various types of artist (chaser, bronze worker, architect, designer and, most of all, sculptor) led on one hand to the appearance of a new figure, that of the workshop master who oversees the creation of works designed by others, and on the other to the proliferation of objects that have practically no functional value and have instead a powerful iconic presence, often sculptural, and are made only for decoration or display. These creations often represent a testing ground in which artisans

exhibitions made a major contribution to the mixing of decorative elements that is at the base of the loss of different and distinctive national styles. The increasingly frequent partnerships

Mirrors

Mirrors with elegant and refined silver frames became very popular during the 18th century, most of them made as part of toilet services. The popularity of mirrors among the aristocracy throughout Europe reflects the style of the period, in which particular importance was given elegance and fashion, with close attention paid the smallest detail. Mirrors in general took on great importance in the homes of the period, for their reflective surfaces (in many cases of Venetian glass) multiplied the lights, colours, and pomp that distinguish the period. Such stylish mirrors were made, albeit in a diminished number, in the course of the 19th century, but these were often weighted down by the excessive decoration typical of that age.

ECLECTICISM

eager to prove the superior quality of handiwork, as accurate as anything machine-made but freer and more imaginative, compete with industrial designers dedicated to reproducing in every tiniest detail the skill of any handicraft and eager to claim equal artistic dignity for their creations. In England, this lively competition led to a heated and intense debate among the various exponents of the culture of the period, among them the designer Henry Cole, the architect and writer Augustus Welby Northmore Pugin, the critic and social theorist John Ruskin, and later the painter and poet William Morris; but the fruit of this competition was quite sterile. The pretense of demonstrating and expressing superior virtuosity, outstanding "art," and technical skill led most often to exhausted exercises, composite, eclectic and heavy, that belie the total

lack of even the slightest effort to define an organic and coherent whole in terms of form and decoration. This situation was aggravated in a large measure by the expansion of the market to embrace broader and increasingly heterogeneous levels of society. The new classes now interested in the acquisition of silver rarely possessed suitable cultural preparation or that refinement of taste that was the prerogative of the rich 18th-century aristocracy. Scarce familiarity with the methods of determining artistic quality led to greater value being given the social significance of silver furnishings, which, burdened by the overloaded decoration that distinguished them, were meant to demonstrate only the social status achieved by their owner. The low quality of execution of many pieces was tolerated, if not unnoticed; indeed, the demand for cast pieces grew, and it

was not important if they were lightweight as long as they were superdecorated.

England in the Victorian age

The tendencies that had appeared in embryonic form during the Regency period—in particular the taste for stylistic revivals and for certain hybrid forms and decorations as well as the proliferation of presentation silver—reached full growth in the Victorian age. The rediscovery of rococo, especially beginning around 1830, was expressed in numerous creations that, although reminiscent of the general form of 18th-century pieces, had no vigour or creative spontaneity and displayed instead a certain weightiness of form with somewhat tired and monotonous decoration. This return to styles of the past became stronger and more general around the middle of the century: chinoiserie came back into fashion and neoclassical and Renaissance themes were repeated and often combined in creations as eclectic as they are burdened with abundant and redundant decoration. There was also the Gothic revival, in large part a result of works by the architect Augustus Welby Northmore Pugin; but his influence in the field of silver was felt most of all in religious pieces. The Victorian age proved a particularly fertile ground for presentation silver, which was produced in great quantities and was used for every possible occasion. In addition to the traditional cups and trophies, silver sculptures were very much in fashion, often created on designs by such leading artists as William Theed or M. C. Wyatt. It was in this genre of object, monumen

tal and heavy, bespeaking the taste, wealth and generosity of the giver, that the inclination for the glowing encomium, the search for expressive complexity, and the taste for the grandiloquent celebration find their highest expression. The same can be said for much of the silver made for display cases; such pieces lost completely any functional value and are simply decorative, often taken, in fact,

as exercises in technical prowess and as such ends in and of themselves. A great many of the most famous examples of presentation silver were made in the workshops of the Garrard company, which in 1843 replaced Rundell Bridge & Rundell as purveyors to the crown. Prince Albert himself commissioned many works from Garrard, some of which he designed himself, such as a celebrated

centerpiece in late-Renaissance style decorated with the figures of the queen's favourite dogs. The London company was well served by Edmund Cotterill, artistic director and tireless producer of models used by many silversmiths. Equally famous was the company founded by George R. Elkington in Birmingham: together with the production of plated pieces it offered objects in silver created with the collaboration of famous French sculptors.

French silver

In France, too, the silver being made at the height of the 19th century showed more concern for literary matters than for sculptural or stylistic intents. The interest in styles of the past did not impede the creation of works instilled with a freedom of composition based on a new inspiration; this was particularly true of pieces of sculptural layout or those made especially for exhibitions: in these the

work of the silversmith and that of the sculptor or artist blend and become as one. The tendency to revive styles of the past had already appeared during the reign of Charles X, when the Gothic enjoyed a return to favour, thanks in part to the work of Cahier, who was not content merely to repeat old forms and decorations but went on to rediscover techniques of medieval art, in particular the use of enamels and filigree. The rediscovery of tra-

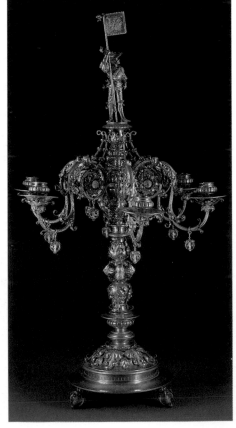

Left: The Shakespeare Vase, by C. F. Hancock to a design by the sculptor Rafael Monti, London, 1864. Shakespeare is the finial; characters from his works appear around the body.

Bottom: Set of four salt cellars with spoons, by S. Smith and W. Nicholson, London, 1862. Each has a figure of a barefoot Sikh with a long mustache, turban and lance.

ditional techniques was a distinguishing mark of much of the silver made during the reign of Louis Philippe (1830-48), when the neo-Gothic gave way to a rising interest in varying shapes and decorations, most of them based on Renaissance stylistic elements. Embossing, chasing and niello found frequent application thanks to work of skilled artisans, among them Antoine Vechte and Charles Wagner.

The influence of the other arts became increasingly tangible, and the leading silversmiths of the period made abundant use of models furnished by decorators, designers, architects and, most of all, sculptors. Such artists as Flagman, Feuchére, Pradier, Cavelier, Preault and Barye often imposed their aesthetic views in three-dimensional shapes and models that silversmiths then had to translate in silver objects. During the reign of Louis Philippe the neorococo style grew steadily in popularity, in large part influenced by the work of Charles Odiot, who had returned from studies and work in England with styles that had already been amplified and affirmed in England. His creations enjoyed great popularity even though their profuse decoration and the certain heaviness of the sculptural pieces were a good distance from the refined 18th-century pieces. The Paris exhibition of 1839 brought to light the man who would become one of the best-known and most-discussed interpreters of 19th-century European silver: François-Désiré Froment-Meurice (1802-55). He enjoyed great prestige although the judgments of his contemporaries were not unanimous; some exalted his virtuosity, even comparing him to Cellini, but there were those who considered him only a good assembler of the work of others. It cannot be denied, however, that many of his works, inspired by sculptural groups by Flagman, Pradier, and Feuchére, display an astonishing mastery of technique. His fame grew enormously and, particularly after the London exhibition of 1851, his three-dimensional works, pervaded by Renaissance stylistic tendencies, were in high demand throughout Europe. Following the interruption in production caused by the February Revolution of 1848, the art of silversmithing came to life again in the period of the Second Republic, during which all the experiences cultivated until then found fulfilment. The interest in antique techniques took new life and was enriched by the frequent use of semiprecious stones and enamels; equally intense was the passion for

the exotic and the Oriental, with the rediscovery of forms and decorations based on Chinese and Japanese art. Together with these tendencies, the 18th-century styles were reevaluated, in particular the neo-classical, for which the Empress Eugenie, Spanish consort of Napoleon III, showed a great deal of constant interest. All these cre-

ations, however, were made following the eclectic inspiration typical of the epoch, so true copies are rare. During this period the works of Charles Christofle (1805-63) found particular fortune. He had begun his activity in a similar vein to that of Froment-Meurice, but early on took a decidedly different route. The Maison Christofle had a certain industrial character, and along with works in sil-

ver made objects of silver with applied plating.

Other European countries

In large part because of the climate of political and social unrest that marked the histories of many European countries during the 19th century, the production of silver underwent a qualitative levelling off that was translated in an uncritical adhesion to his-

Hallmarks of 19th-century Russian master silversmiths

Egorov Dmitrij
Aleksandrovich

Pets Kostantin
Jakovlevich

Ovchinnikov
Pavel Akimov

Sazikov Pavel
Fedorovich

Ivan Ekimovich
Morosov

Sev'er Aleksandr
Tomas

Ovchinnikov Ivan
Ivanovich

Lockytov
Petr

Alekseev Ivan
Aleksejevich

Zolpin
Nicolaj

Juden
Adam

Mitin Aleksandr
Nikolaevech

Opposite above: Coffeepot by Johan Heinoin, St. Petersburg, 1876. The cone-shaped body has an S-shaped spout and is decorated with motifs of the "old Russia" style.

Opposite below: Ewer with cover made in Moscow, 1862. Both the shape and decoration recall Oriental models.

Below: Kovsch (wine bowl), Moscow, end 19th century. Having progressively lost their original function, such objects were given symbolic importance and were used as gifts.

Bottom: Tankard made in Russia, 1880. The cylindrical body stands on three feet and is decorated with a troika, the typical three-horse sled or carriage of Russia.

toricism and spreading eclecticism.

English and French models, spread by way of that great promotion vehicle, the international exhibition, influenced the silver made in other countries, and together with the common tendency for marked monumentality, there was the rediscovery of styles from the past, which were reinterpreted and combined with little coherence and without any concern of obtaining even a minimal sense of expressive homogeneity. The various pieces made are sometimes distinguished by the quality of their execution, but nothing more. The Gothic revival style was often used in the creation of objects for liturgical use, and these works are sometimes remarkable.

Russia

Against the background of general monotony found in European silver of this period, a certain spark of originality can be seen in some of the silver pieces made in Russia. In Russia as elsewhere, many artisans were affected by the eclectic tendency, and the influence of European models is clear in much work, most of all from St. Petersburg. Of course, by then, Russian silver, most of all display plate, was traditionally and historically tied to Western tradition, in particular to that of

157

Below: Cup with handle made in Russia, 1896. The embossed silver body is shaped like a basket. Initials are applied to the front.

Bottom: Bucket in silver, Moscow, 1887. The simple cone shape is interrupted only by two series of bomé bands; the handle is hinged to both sides of the upper border.

Left: Throne salt cellar in gilt silver, Kostroma 1908-17. The back of the throne is pierced with geometric motifs; the seat is a hinged cover.

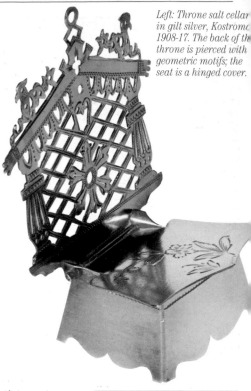

Germany and France. The rulers and aristocracy usually commissioned their services directly from the most celebrated masters working in European cities, Augsburg and Paris in particular. Perhaps as a reaction to this situation of cultural dependence, an artistic movement guided by various artists, patrons, and intellectuals began around the middle of the 19th century; known as the Slavic revival, this movement sought to revitalize Russia's artistic traditions. Most of all in Moscow, numerous pieces were made based on inspiration taken from traditional forms with a rediscovery of indigenous decoration. The *bratine* (fraternity cups) *kovsch* (vessels for mixing wine or beer) and the other traditional types of Russian culture met with vast popularity. This movement was given great support by Peter Carl Fabergé (1846-1920) who, in addition to his exceptional *objets de vertu* and his production marked by a form of the neorococo that anticipated certain themes soon to be attributed to Art Nouveau, made numerous objects in the "old Russia" style.

Throne salt cellars

In eastern European countries, the act of greeting guests was given a ritual character of great traditional importance. The essential elements for the ceremonial rite were bread, salt and wine. The bread and salt, in particular, were part of a ritual procedure that required a basket for the bread and a container for the salt. In the homes of the aristocracy or those of the rich middle class, such containers were of silver. Silver baskets complete with silver tablecloths are known, although they are rare. Salt cellars in the shape of small chairs were very widespread. The high, pierced backs of these explain why they have come to be called throne salt cellars. The seat enclosed the salt. Engraved on the face of the seat was a phrase of greetings or the owner's coat of arms and initials.

159

CITY	STANDARD	ANNUAL LETTERS				
LONDON		K	e	F	O	P
		from A 1796 to U 1815	from A 1816 to U 1835	from A 1836 to U 1855	from A 1856 to U 1875	from A 1876 to U 1895
YORK		d	O	g	F	K
		from A 1787 to Z 1811	from A 1787 to Z 1811	from A 1812 to Z 1836	from A 1837 to V 1856	from A 1837 to V 1856
EXETER		F	h	B	L	E
		from A 1797 to U 1816	from A 1817 to U 1836	from A 1837 to U 1856	from A 1857 to U 1876	from A 1877 to F 1882
NEWCASTLE		X	Q	J	g	l
		from A 1791 to Z 1814	from A 1815 to Z 1838	from A 1839 to Z 1863	from A 1864 to U 1883	from A 1864 to U 1883
CHESTER		M	S	R	d	B
		from A 1797 to V 1817	from A 1818 to U 1838	from A 1839 to Z 1863	from A 1864 to U 1883	from A 1884 to R 1900
BIRMINGHAM		P	E	T	u	y
		from A 1824 to Z 1848	from A 1849 to Z 1874	from A 1849 to Z 1874	from A 1875 to Z 1899	from A 1900 to Z 1924
SHEFFIELD		w	q	T	M	
		from E 1800 to U 1823	from A 1824 to Z 1843	from A 1844 to Z 1867	from A 1868 to Z 1892	from A 1893 to Z 1917
EDINBURGH		N	r	T	S	m
		from A 1780 to Z 1805	from A 1806 to Z 1831	from A 1832 to Z 1856	from A 1857 to Z 1881	from A 1882 to Z 1905
GLASGOW		R	M	G	A	N
		from A 1819 to Z 1844	from A 1845 to Z 1870	from A 1871 to Z 1896	from A 1897 to Z 1922	from A 1897 to Z 1922
DUBLIN		T	O	t	Z	A
		from A 1797 to Z 1820	from A 1821 to Z 1845	from A 1846 to Z 1870	from A 1871 to Z 1895	from A 1896 to U 1915

20TH-CENTURY SILVER

Proto-Art Nouveau
Art Nouveau
Art Deco
Post-Art Deco
The 1940s
The 1950s

PROTO-ART NOUVEAU

The proto-Art Nouveau

The leading style of the period from 1890 to 1907, which is known by many names—*Sezessionstil* (Austria), *Jugendstil* (Germany), *Floreale* or Liberty (Italy), *Modernismo* (Spain), and Art Nouveau (the last being the most commonly accepted)—did not evolve overnight. Many cultural forces and trends contributed to its birth and development, first among them probably the burning desire to break free of the ties and bonds of the eclectic style, which forced a continuous revival of obso-

Tiffany

Interior decorator, painter, designer and creator of silver, glass and jewels, Louis Comfort Tiffany (1848-1933) was one of the most multi-talented and creative people active in the world of the decorative and applied arts in the period between the 19th and 20th centuries. Louis Comfort was born into an artistic family; his father, Charles Lewis (1812-1902), founded Tiffany & Co., which soon became famous for its jewellery, and he made improvements to the style of silverware that won wide recognition; Tiffany products gained prestige and fame at various international exhibitions. Louis Comfort first studied in the United States and then went to Paris; his interests soon turned to decoration and were greatly influenced by the study of exotic objects with E. C. Moore, future director of Tiffany & Co. and a great collector; Louis Comfort never copied such models but used them as a source of continuous inspiration for the creation of highly original objects, often permeated by Oriental and Islamic suggestions. In 1879 he founded the interior-decorating firm in New York that came to be known as Tiffany Studios, dedicated primarily to furnishings; in 1882 he was asked to redecorate the White House. He is perhaps most famous for his work in glass, but his many activities included designs for jewellery and silver, which were made in the Tiffany & Co. factories and enjoyed great success.

Left: The Goelet Cup, 1885 silver trophy for the winner of a regatta, Tiffany & Co., New York, 1885. Shaped like a ewer, this is richly decorated with various motifs.

Bottom: Pitcher made partially of silver by William Wilson & Son, Philadelphia, final decade 19th century. The body is embossed and chased to present a pond with applied turtle decoration.

talizing of art in general. Naturally this idealization of the artisan, of production done entirely by hand, came into conflict with the use of factory processes in artistic endeavours. The cult of the line and of movement was spread by the designs of Christopher Dresser (1834-1904) in which the curved line is based on logical and geometric orders, as in the case of the curving ellipsoid line with three centers that remained the typical model of Art Nouveau stylistic elements. The innovators of this pioneering period were convinced that the more complex a curved line was the more beautiful it was. It is important to note that interest in the decorative qualities of sinuous lines was related to the twining of tendrils in the organic growth of plants, and this paved the way for an extraordinary variety of ornamental motifs based on the lines and shapes of plants.

Another great stimulus to the growth of Art Nouveau came from the artistic works of the English artist and poet William Blake (1757-1827), most of all from the illustrations for his books that he himself made. Even today, the long, twisting tongues of flames that deco-

lete stylistic elements from the past. This powerful longing to be free of the shapes and decorations of the past led to a yearning for creativity imbued with imagination and expressive liberty, and this in turn suggested an approach based on direct and immediate inspiration drawn from "nature." Other important and innovative ideas came from the doctrines put forward by the leaders of the English Pre-Raphaelite and Arts and Crafts movements, John Ruskin (1819-1900) and William Morris (1834-96) respectively. For both men the notion of equality among the arts was based principally on decorative artisan work and on its renewal, which would necessarily bring about a revi-

rate his texts—his celebrated "fire flowers," which date from around 1789—seem astonishing, and these can be considered the earliest anticipation of Art Nouveau. Blake's illustrations became widely known only after an exhibition held in 1876; his influence reached the Art Nouveau style by way of the works of the Pre-Raphaelite movement, which began in England in 1848.

Another aspect of the period must be given due consideration: the influence of Orientalism. Around 1863 collecting Japanese *objets d'art* became vastly popular, and their close relationship to plant elements, detailed painted backgrounds and

incessantly moving forms found wide applications in the graphic arts, in ceramics and in silver well before the establishment of Art Nouveau.

There was also the multi-talented Walter Crane (1845-1915), designer, illustrator of children's books, painter, art critic and "proto-industrial designer." He made a noticeable contribution to the early development of Art Nouveau, most of all during the years 1860-80. In his graphic works and in particular in the volume of designs for carpets *Lines and Outlines*, published in 1875, he presented a broad range of motifs characterized by

stylized flowers. These were quite distant from the naturalism in style during those years, but they were later drawn on during the mature period of the Art Nouveau.

Art Nouveau

Some of Art Nouveau's great appeal results from the fact that it was an artistic movement primarily related to the applied and decorative arts—furniture and jewellery, book design and illustration, as well as silver and other domestic ware—and indeed it puts them on the same level as the figurative arts.

Art Nouveau evolved slow-

Flower vase in silver, Budapest, early 20th century. The oval body rests on four elaborately scrolled feet and has two side figures bearing musical instruments.

ly in England, with its earliest signs in the Arts and Crafts movement; on the Continent, however, the new style blossomed suddenly around 1890: in Belgium and then in Holland, in France, in Germany, Austria and Italy. It was also popular in Scotland and the United States. The style's period of greatest development is usually said to be the years 1895-1902, when it was applied throughout Europe in every field of artistic activity. That this was the style's apex is supported by the fact nearly a hundred new magazines on art were published during the 1890s; the pages of these

---

ART NOUVEAU MOTIFS

The Art Nouveau style changed from place to place but showed a common tendency towards expression in which the decoration was an integral part of the form. The use of plant-inspired motifs was constant, even though the strong tendency for stylization often renders these quite unintelligible. The motifs were curvilinear and sinuous in rhythms measured off by accentuated ribbing and by a continuous, light line. Curling lines are often interspersed by structural knots that take the form of floral crowns or capricious interweavings. Also recurrent are female heads with flowing hair or wings.

ART NOUVEAU

Below: Fish platter, embossed and chased with stylized motifs of branches, leaves and buds. Embossed and chased flowers are applied at the sides. Austria, end of the 19th century.

Bottom: One of a pair of trays, embossed, chased and partially pierced. The angles are decorated with flowers, fruits and branches. Austro-Hungarian Empire, end of the 19th century.

This consists of a succession of asymmetrical curves that give a sense of powerful movement, full of energy. The models presented by the Scottish school are refined, in a style that is linear and two-dimensional; those from Belgium are intensely dynamic with movement based on a typical well-structured countermovement; in France particular use was made of intertwining lines and plant motifs; in Germany and the Austrian Vienna school straight and constructive lines were preferred. Beyond such general aspects, when this decoration was applied to such three-dimensional objects as silver, it took on a profoundly different meaning. With such pieces the line grows relentlessly, delicately twisting and wrapping around the form of the object until it becomes one

magazines express a shared longing for renewal of the arts and a new interest in the applied arts. Based on an ideological stance, this style is an ornamental style based principally on the continuous curving line.

HALLMARKS OF THE MASTER SILVER-SMITHS OF WIENER WERKSTÄTTE

The characteristic trait of the hallmarks used by the artists working in these silver workshops was that they were either initials inserted in a circular form or were circular forms created by initials. Standing out among the many silversmiths were Adolf Erbrich, Josef Hossfeld, Alfred Mayer, and Josef

 Josef Hossfeld

 Karl Kallert

 Josef Czech

 Adolf Erbrich

 Augustin Grötzbach

 Josef Husnik

 Alfred Mayer

 Josef Wagner

Wagner. Among many other works, Erbrich is known for a coffeepot in silver and ebony and several boxes of hammered silver, all made on designs by Hoffmann. Hossfeld made silvers in the modern style on designs by Moser. Mayer, too, is known for works in silver and lapis lazuli designed by Moser. Wagner produced centerpieces and table cigarette boxes designed by Hoffmann.

Wiener Werkstätte

*The Wiener Werkstätte
("Viennese workshops") was
an association for the production of objects designed by the
leading artists and made by
the most skilled artisans active
in Vienna. It was founded in
1903 by the architect Josef
Hoffmann, the designer Kilo
Moser, and the banker Fritz
Waerndorfer with the aim of
renewing and reorganizing
the production of artisan
crafts, which had been com-
promised by industrial mass
production. The workshops
produced furniture, silver,
jewels, fabrics, porcelain, wallpaper, mosaics and bookbindings. Until it closed in 1932,
the Wiener Werkstätte produced works whose beautiful
designs and technical artistry
placed them in the forefront of
European production.*

with it. This decoration is always alive and animated, but at the same time it is balanced, capable of empha-sizing the overall balance of the forms and presenting this harmony as the protago-nist of the piece.

Outside England, Art Nouveau came to present four different formal approaches, including the dynamic one of Belgium, that inspired by the plant world in France, the two-dimensional forms of the Scottish school and finally the geometric-constructive forms of Germany and Austria.

ART NOUVEAU

The Vienna school

Two kinds of silver were made in Austria. The first had intensely curvilinear decoration that was, however, flat, barely raised, and closely connected to the surface of the object. Emblematic of this type are the many elegant and refined trays that decorated almost all the middle-class homes of Vienna and the other cities of the Austrian empire. The other type, which was highly important, involved a continuous movement stressing the tendency towards expression based on squares, circles and straight lines. In this decorative repertory, even the symbolic meaning of flowers, for example, was reduced by vigorous geome-

try to essential forms. Without doubt, Vienna's geometric Art Nouveau represented an extreme version of the movement; indeed, it can be said to have foreshadowed stylistic trends of the 1920s and 1930s. Performed in the celebrated Wiener Werkstätte applied-arts workshops, the production of silver was part of the large cultural movement of the Vienna Secession, which was organized in 1897 by the painter Gustav Klimt (1862-1918) together with other artists, including the architects Josef Hoffmann (1870-1956) and Josef Maria Olbrich (1867-1908).

Two new art magazines, *Kunst und Kunsthandwerk*, dedicated to the applied arts and furnish-

ings, and *Ver Sacrum*, the highly sophisticated official organ of the Secession, provided a wealth of models for the movement. The designs for the works in silver produced by the artisans of the Wiener Werkstätte were prepared by Josef Hoffman, the great graphic designer Koloman Moser (1868-1918), the architect Otto Prutscher (1880-1949), and

Opposite top: One of a pair of silver vases, London, 1903. The tapering body decorated with repeating floral motifs rises from a shaped base.

Opposite bottom: Tea service by Jean Puiforcat, France, early 20th century. The sugar bowl, cream pitcher, teapot and water pitcher are all decorated with floral motifs.

Below and bottom: Front and back of a centerpiece made and signed by Vincenzo Gemito (1852-1929) in Naples, 1925. The embossed silver convex body is decorated on one side with two dol-

phins and on the other by a wreath of intertwined roses and a diadem. Attached to the sides are the heads of children with hair of flowers, leaves, and fruit.

Jean Puiforcat

Jean Puiforcat (Paris, 1897-1945) is the most famous French silversmith of the 20th century. Born into the business (the Puiforcat workshop dates back to 1820), he began working for his father in 1920, having fought in the "Legion of the Thousand" during the First World War. His early work displayed no particular distinguishing features, being partly inspired by the "modern style" and partly by a search for new shapes that anticipated Art Deco. From 1925, when he exhibited some hundred pieces at the world-famous Exposition des Arts Décoratifs in Paris with considerable success, the shapes of his creations became increasingly pure, with a rejection of straight lines along with any sort of unnecessary decoration: he preferred, rather, to combine silver with semiprecious stones like lapis lazuli, jade, onyx, and aventurine. In 1928 he joined the Union des Artistes Modernes, founded by René Herbst under the slogan "imposer le beau dans l'utile." Their first exhibition was held in 1930; the pieces shown by Puiforcat proclaimed the growing importance of curving lines and an increasingly imaginative association of silver with such materials as ebonite, glass, crystal, fluorite, marble and alabaster, with the result that many critics identify this period as being the one in which the stylistic elements of Art Deco were abandoned and the so-called rétro style was born. At the 1937 exhibition Puiforcat introduced vermeil gilding: objects were dominated by curving lines and displayed growing concern for the relationship between form and function.

the painter and designer Carl Otto Czeshka (1878-1960). The Vienna school preferred simple forms in which the play of piercing participated in the general context and in which the decorative theme was insistently repeated in such a way as to become an essential part of the form. The most popular types of silver objects were boxes, made with endless imagination in myriad shapes, vases, table stands, samovars, coffeepots

and centerpieces. An important aspect of these pieces is that some include portions not made of silver but instead of such coloured materials as lapis lazuli, cornelian, yellow amber, ivory and bright enamels.

Austria was the last country to appear on the world panorama of Art Nouveau silver and was also the first to break with Art Nouveau; as early as the years 1906-8 Austrian silversmiths were experimenting with com-

ART NOUVEAU

pletely new forms that anticipated those later identified with Art Deco.

French Art Nouveau silver

Remarkable works in silver were made in France during this period, characterized by high levels of quality, keen stylistic homogeneity, and the contributions of worthy artists. The creation of this silver reflects the economic and social conditions of France at the turn of the century. The new rising and dominant class was com-posed by the rich bour-geoisie, enlightened and open to innovation in all fields of artistic creativity. Most of all in Paris, people were particularly aware of new movements and trends in fashion. Art Nouveau, pre-sented as a style of ele-gance, was thus in a posi-tion to give a mark of quality to all products of the applied arts, and silver, in particular, proved equal to the task. Indeed, by remain-ing within the highest tradi-tions of refined French craftsmanship, the Art Nouveau silver of Paris was able to present completely acceptable novelties. In this

regard, particular attention goes to the works made by the house of Christofle, in particular the models based on designs by Lucien Falize, which show a preference for forms and decorations taken directly from nature. Among the other artists working for Christofle were Joseph-François Joindy, Arnoux, Léon Mallet and René Rozet. Rozet is well-represented by a typically Art Nouveau centerpiece dedicated to air and water and made of silver and milk glass with ivory figures, all of it a triumph of curved lines. Arnoux made vases in simple forms with elegant floral decoration as well as numerous silver services composed of several pieces. The works made at Christofle reflect both the presence of Arnoux, who was in charge of works in modern art at Christofle, and the enlightened artistic direction of Henri Bouilhet and André Bouilhet, grand-son and great grandson of the founder of the company, Charles Christofle. Among the most prolific silver-smiths of this period were André Aucoc, Placide Poussielgue-Rusand, the Falize brothers, Ernest

Cardeilhac and Debain. The works by Aucoc show a certain tradition tied to 18th-century models but are directed, perhaps as a result of his friendship with René Lalique, at an Art Nouveau inspired by the examples of Lucien Falize. The works of Placide Poussielgue-Rusand were completed, beginning in 1889, by his son Maurice, who carried on the monumentality traditional to his father, but added to his works a well-balanced quantity of motifs in clear imitation of nature, such as flow-

ers, vines and olive leaves, all presented in the sinuous movement preferred by the new style. Cardeilhac was distinguished for interesting silver mounts made for ceramic vases; their fluid lines, graceful movement, and stylized plant elements combine to present a highly personal interpretation of the Art Nouveau style. In this sense, this artist, who died in 1904 at only fifty-three years of age, can be seen as an innovator who approached the light forms of the Art Deco style. The works of Debain, made impressive by the use of floral decoration on a grand scale, are often indebted to models furnished by Arnoux.

The three Falize brothers—André, Jean, and Pierre—formed a harmonious group of silversmiths. After the premature death of their father, Lucien, they

Cup in parcel-gilt silver with enamelling, by Tiffany & Co., New York, first half 20th century. The three-lobed amphora-shape body has three handles decorated with stylized flowers and leaves.

divided among themselves the running of his workshop, one of the most important in Paris. Jean was the administrator, Pierre a skilled designer, and André an exceptional artist. Their studio produced the most important silver and jewels of this period, and they came to boast the most exclusive clientele: Czar Nicholas II, marshals of France, the queen of Rumania, and so on. The essential characteristic of their work resulted from their taking the flower as their principal source of inspiration, but there was more: they also made use of the motif of large leaves

wrapped around the bases of vases or the bodies of tureens, and they also employed the lizard motif, so widespread and dear to jewellery-making.

Russian silver

Russian silver of the Art Nouveau period can be divided into three types: fashionable works based on models from western Europe, works inspired by traditional Oriental motifs, and the "aristocratic" works from the Fabergé studio. For western models, the Russians turned most often to those from Paris, not surprising given the Russian

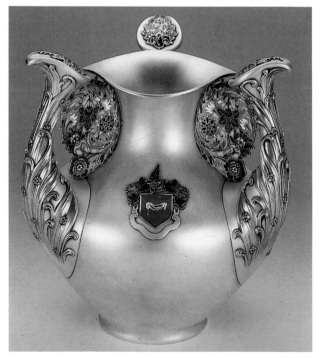

Georg Jensen

Georg Jensen (1866-1935) worked as a sculptor and ceramist before dedicating himself to silversmithing, first in the workshop of Mogens Ballin and then in his own workshop in Copenhagen, which he opened in 1904. Beginning in 1910 Jensen's works earned international fame, partly a result of his participation in many exhibitions at which he acquired prestigious recognition. To meet the increasing number of requests for his work, Jensen founded a new factory, Georg Jensen Sølvsmedie, in 1918, the only one in the world dedicated exclusively to the production of modern silver. Jensen was able to combine artisan methods with industrial production systems and wisely surrounded himself with highly qualified collaborators, first among them Johan Rohde (1856-1935). Painter, sculptor, architect and designer, Rohde began supplying designs to the Danish factory in 1905 and became a permanent member in 1913. Aside from Rohde, other contributors included Harald Nielsen (who became artistic director of the company on Jensen's death), Gundorph Albertus, Arno Malinowsky, and Gundlach Pedersen. The stylistic traits of these various designers often can be recognized in the works from Jensen Sølvsmedie.

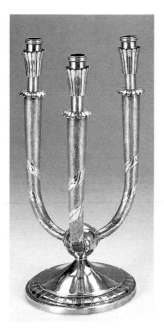

admiration in general for things French (French was spoken at the court of the czars). Of greater interest are the works in silver in which Oriental curved lines and superdecoration of vines were transformed into works composed of hemispheres, leafed coils and flowers in forms that were almost always compact and solid. The strictly Art Nouveau works of Fabergé are principally vases mounted in silver, in which stems and leaves wrap lightly around pieces expressed in deliciously sinuous lines. Fabergé turned to the skills of the artisan V. Aarne for these mountings. In other cases, such typically Russian objects as the *kovsh* and *bratine* were transformed through the application of Art Nouveau stylistic motifs to the original forms, particularly handles. Fabergé also made naturalistic table dec-orations using leaves and the lizard motif.

The first signs of Art Deco

While Art Nouveau was still at the height of its popularity, albeit in a waning stage, the first notable signs appeared of a large movement directed at both changing its stylistic traits and proposing completely new forms and decorations. Rather than achieving the predicted rejuvenation of Art Nouveau taste, the "great international exposition of decorative and industrial arts" held in Turin in 1902 marked the decline of Art Nouveau, at least in terms of the most important expressions of formal style.

173

ART DECO

Fruit bowl in hammered silver by Georg Jensen, Denmark, 1915-19. The cup is supported by shaped cylindrical columns; the juncture between cup and columns is decorated with leaves and berries.

Examples were presented in the field of the applied arts that were completely detached from the past and of enormous interest for the future. There is no trace whatsoever of Art Nouveau

in the famous two-branched candelabrum with inserted amethysts designed by the architect Josef Maria Olbrich and produced by P. Bruckmann & Son of Heilbronn circa 1901. The

same is true of the electric kettle produced by the powerful German company AEG around 1908 based on a design by the architect Peter Behrens (1868-1940), a fundamental figure among the pioneers of modern architecture and industrial design. During the first decade of the 20th century the German design school asserted itself with innovative models spread through studios located in various cultural centers, such as the Vereinigten Werkstätten für Kunst im Handwerk in Munich, the Künstlerkolonie in Darmstadt, and several studios in Berlin. In terms of works in silver, many designs were made by Hans Christiansen (1866-1945); Paul Haustein (1880-1944) made experiments combining translucent enamels with silver in rigidly symmetrical geometric forms; and following

ART DECO MOTIFS

A discussion of the decorative repertory of the aesthetic movement known as Art Deco is rendered difficult by the movement's complexity. It cannot be denied that each object was made to serve a clear and purposeful ornamental function; indeed, this decorative aspect was the result of a great deal of research. It is, however, quite difficult to distinguish those decorative motifs that are typical

and peculiar only to a single artist or group of artists working within a particular cultural area from those that can be considered widespread, recurrent elements found in all the production of silver of the first thirty years of the 20th century. Many of the models were based on or derived from the fervid investigations into form and decoration carried out by groups of avant-garde artists. Some of the decora-

tive motifs in the period seem based on inspiration drawn from the cubists, for example; these are distinguished by a tendency toward the geometric, the linear, the symmetrical.

designs by Albin Müller (1871-1941), the Koch & Bergfeld Co. of Bremen made stark, highly stylized coffee services in completely smooth silver raised only by subtle bands of geometric decoration. The new style made itself felt in lines that went from being sinuous to being straight; the iris surrendered the field to the rose, which is the flower best suited to geometrization; and the fantastically, almost uncontrollably intertwining curves gave way to the rigours of squares and the compass. Not the least of the reasons for the movement from Art Nouveau to Art Deco was the fact that handicrafts had been finally vanquished by industrial methods, and criteria involving a close attention to economy began to take over: quite simply, the straight line is more economical than the sinuous. A new "symbol" was needed, one that would indicate the change in style and make it more appealing as a status symbol to the great mass of middle class still immersed in the Art Nouveau style. Curiously, the final push for the change in styles came from an imaginative Parisian tailor, Paul Poiret, who as early as 1906 launched the "simple and straight line":

Other decorative elements are based on more traditional schemes, such as the plant world, but these show a marked tendency for stylization, repetition, and odd mixtures in enclosed, symmetrical compositions. A great deal of Art Deco silver makes use of chromatic or material contrasts; never before had combinations of different materials been so exploited for decorative ends. Lacquers and enamels were

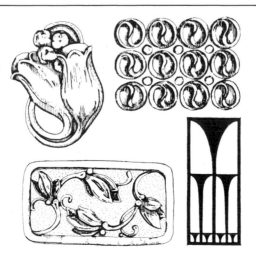

often used to colour various parts of a piece; even more common is the combination of silver surfaces—smooth, opacified, or hammered—with such varied materials as glass, plastic, exotic woods, or semi-precious stones, including onyx, alabaster, jade, quartz, or lapis lazuli, which are often shaped or moulded to better construct secondary parts, such as handles and finials.

Below: Coffee service in silver and ivory designed by Johan Rohde in 1919 for the Georg Jensen Sølvsmedie; the service includes a coffeepot, sugar bowl and creamer.

Bottom: Samovar in silver with bone handle made by J. D. Klinkosch, France, 1930s. The geometric form presents a faceted profile with fourteen vertical bands.

this came to mean essential, geometric, square—in keeping with the modern.

Art Deco silver

Unlike the creations of pure art and even the products

of many other areas of the applied arts, Art Deco silver encountered a good deal of resistance and had trouble establishing itself since it tended to present models based on the eclectic period inspired by past centuries and since the models proposed by leading designers did not meet with enough approval to justify large-scale production. From the chronological point of view, Art Deco silver arrived late, during the 1920s, whereas other categories of art objects along with illustration had begun around 1909-10. This is also a result of the First World War; the war left most Europeans with little money to spend on luxuries, and only during the 1920s did people again turn to spending on objects made of precious metals. The shapes of the objects

are based on "pure" forms: spheres, rhombuses, cubes, polygons, ovals and pyramidal constructions. Motifs based on the plant or animal world are presented using extremely stylized structures. The quite legitimate question arose as to whether the shapes of silver were not, at least in part, inspired by such new artistic fashions as cubism, futurism, abstractism and fauvism. In 1908 the famous Austrian architect Adolf Loos (1870-1933), guiding light of the modern movement, wrote: "Today, thanks to modern progress, objects have no need of decoration, and any decoration applied to an object only spoils that object's functional capacities and is a profanation of its material." Even so, the demand for "decorated" items was too intense on

Tea and coffee service with tray by the Wiener Werkstätte, designed by Josef Hoffmann, c. 1920. The containers have segmented radial convex bodies and ivory handles and finials.

the part of buyers to persuade silversmiths to give it up completely. Loos's pronouncement was heeded only in the 1930s, and even then against much resistance. To question of decoration was best answered by the works of the well-known silversmiths of the period: Georg Jensen (1866-1935) and Jean Puiforcat (1897-1945). Jensen's early works are somewhat sober, marked only by rounded edges and hammered surfaces. He later developed a completely original style based on objects embellished with abundant decoration with spires, bunches of flowers and fruit, grape clusters and garlands in contrast to the surfaces of simple, linear forms. In the 1920s, Puiforcat created pieces tied more to function than decoration: the most interesting of these are his tea and coffee services, plates and cups. The characteristic these share is that they are based on simple rectangular or cylindrical forms enriched by finials of jade, ivory, lapis lazuli, or precious woods. In the 1930s his style became increasingly essential, with daring flared lines in which the volume of the piece is given the most emphasis. The taste for geometricized animal forms appears in some of the silver made by Christofle, including wonderful sweetmeat dishes in the shape of stylized "futuristic" squirrels designed by Cazès and sauceboats in the shape of swans with the spoon in the shape of the head and neck of the bird designed in simple and essential forms by Fjerdingstd. In Austria,

Josef Hoffmann

Born in Pirnitz in Moravia in 1870, Josef Hoffmann studied architecture at Vienna and in 1892 became assistant to the famous Viennese architect Otto Wagner. He was a member of the Vienna Secession, was among the founders in 1903 of the Wiener Werkstätte, and in 1912 helped found the Österreichische Werkbund. In addition to his intense activity as an architect and creator of important expositions, he was a fecund designer, designing metal, silver, jewels, glass, ceramics, furniture, lamps, bookbindings, fabrics and wallpaper and forming the backbone of an independent style the influenced almost all the artistic production of Vienna early in the century. Initially hostile to all decoration, he later adopted geometric forms, preferring the square and rectangle. His forms passed from severity to free, dynamic movement. He died in Vienna in 1956.

Centerpiece with cover in silver and jade by A. Lapara, France, 1925-27. The octagonal body has two ring handles and two cylindrical holders in jade.

Opposite bottom: Centerpiece in silver by Jean Puiforcat, France, c. 1930. The four short faces of the octagonal body have jade handles attached by silver elements.

silversmiths preferred flaring and fluted forms and broad swellings reminiscent of rose buds, skilfully interspersed by piercing. Rounded elements are often joined using a characteristic spiralling motif called the spring. Among the outstanding Viennese silversmiths was Dagobert Pêche (1887-1923), who began working with the Wiener Werkstätte in 1915 and whose pieces are distinguished by a characteristic layout. He repeated and further developed motifs inspired by flowers, large leaves and berries, interspersing these with broad areas of gadrooning. A similar layout can be seen in the silver objects made on designs by Otto Prutscher.

A wide range of contributions to the field of silver was made by the production houses of Jensen and the International Silver Co., as well as by the designer Weber. The Danish firm of Jensen began its activity in 1904 with its founder, Georg Jensen, and expanded to have important branches in Paris, London and New York, offering a vast and famous line. The most popular of these were coffee and tea sets, series of candlesticks, candelabra, tureens, cocktail shakers, table cigarette boxes and innumerable types of luxury *objets d'art*. The silver made by the American Karl Emmanuel Martin Weber (1889-1963) is character-

ized by rigorous, almost metaphysical, volumes much in keeping with the ideas of modern movements in Germany, including several references to the celebrated Bauhaus style. Weber was extremely active as a designer of models, especially from 1927 on, and the Friedman Silver Co. and International Silver Co. both made much use of his designs. The International Silver Co., active from 1898 to 1984, specialized in the 1920s and 1930s in the production of modern silver for luxury hotels and boasted, among other creations, the invention of tea services made of several elements that could be assembled to form a single unit.

Post-Deco, or the 1930s

On July 18, 1925, the *Exposition Internationale des Arts Décoratifs et Industriels Modernes* opened in Paris. This celebration of the state of the applied arts at the end of the first quarter of the century attracted so much attention that the style of the period was given a name based on the exposition's title: Art Deco, from *Arts Décoratifs*. Thus the style had a name; but just as the 1902 Turin exhibition had marked the end of the style it was meant to celebrate, Art Nouveau, the 1925 Paris exhibition that gave Art Deco its name came to mark that style's downfall. The exhibition did confirm an important concept: the applied arts had been fully accepted into the world of art production, with no distinction made between objects made for use and those of pure aesthetic pleasure. The time was ripe for the new contributions that eventually led to the overcoming of Art Deco. In the same year, 1925, the Bauhaus moved to Dessau, and the rationalist movement began offering its long-awaited fruits. The teachings of Làszlo Moholy-Nagy, a leading member of the Bauhaus, led to free invention with forms rigorously treated using rhythms and mathematical and geometric proportions all in accordance with a quest for the essential. In terms of works in metal, this meant kettles, teapots and lamps of absolute efficiency in forms that were solidly geometric. Without doubt, the teachings of the Bauhaus had effects on the silver made during the 1930s. It is indicative of this that the Deutscher Werkbund, directed by the architect Walter Gropius, also director of the Bauhaus, was invited to display objects at the 20th Salon of decorative arts in Paris. All this innovative ferment was reflected in silver objects of extreme rigour. Outstanding examples of this are the salt shakers designed by Luc Lanel and produced by

POST-DECO

Below: Tea service in silver and ivory designed by Jean Tétard for Tétard Frères, France, c. 1930. Each piece is composed of two matched oval elements on a rectangular base.

Opposite bottom: Tea and coffee service by the Italian architect Antonio Sant'Elia, c. 1930. The smooth surfaces are marked off by rings broken by geometric spouts tight to the body.

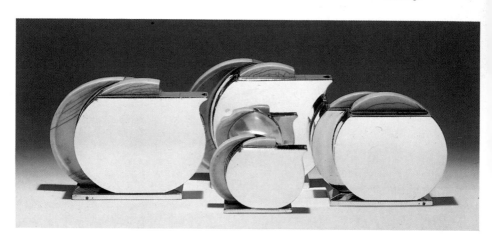

Christofle for the tables of the transatlantic cruise ship *Normandie*: these are perfect spheres with engraved at the center a five-pointed star with six flowers between the points. Also typical are the cylindrical ice buckets, the lower part of which is ringed by light bands, and the handles of which are fluted wings. The object given most prestige during the 1930s was the silver tea service, an object of importance to middle-class families eager to have an attractive piece in their dining room. These were composed of four pieces: teapot, sugar bowl, milk pitcher and box to hold used tea leaves. The preferred form was a parallelepiped with slightly curving sides and a spout only barely projecting from the upper border. Rigorous geometry was applied to handles and the finials of covers: quarter cylinders, whole cylinders standing on a parallelepiped, spheres and cubes. Handles and finials were made of wood or ivory and sometimes in galalite or bakelite. The models based on designs by Jean Puiforcat and Gérard Sandoz took the geometric aspect to extreme conse-

ART DECO HANDLES

One of the characteristic elements of the tea and coffee services of the first years of the 20th century is the handle. Thanks in part to the use of such varied materials as semiprecious stones, exotic woods, glass, plastic and ivory, many designers were able to give their creations handles with sharply defined profiles constructed geometrically and marked by a harmonious continuity of form.

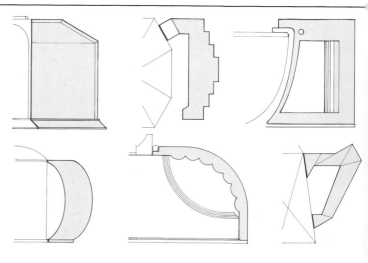

quences; it is revealing that the designs were made entirely using ruler and compass without the least bit of free-hand drawing: absolute precision. Some objects of display plate, particularly centerpieces, dessert baskets and ornamental vases, are pervaded by the drive to seem monumental. Broad, smooth surfaces are divided in panels of inclined planes that give the impression of forms taken from architectural decoration or, as in the case of large vases in the style of flared chalices, of translations in silver of glass vases.

Another recurrent element is a particular stepped design that seems related to the uppermost part of Aztec temples; this element enjoyed great favour among American silversmiths. An interesting aspect of the silver pieces of this period is the carefully balanced contrast between the metal and other materials. This was in a period of extreme rationalism, and the use of these materials instead of silver was tied directly to function. Of course, wood had been used for the handles of tea- and coffeepots as early as the 18th century to protect the hand from heat, and wood remained the favoured material, but use was also made or rare, exotic woods, particularly those brightly coloured. Also used was ivory, which combined both precious beauty and insulating qualities. The most typical of this period, however, are handles and other parts made of such materials as bakelite, a new kind of plastic much used in the 1930s, although it was rarely expressly requested by the buyers of silver, since it was looked upon as a "poor" material not worthy of associating with the likes of a "rich" material like silver. It should also be pointed out that these materials lent themselves to plastic modeling and were thus well-adapted to solving the problem of obtaining big volumes—large bodies— that were also lightweight.

In an age of famous designers and fashionable manufacturers, it is not surprising that hallmarks were sometimes joined by names written out entirely, such as

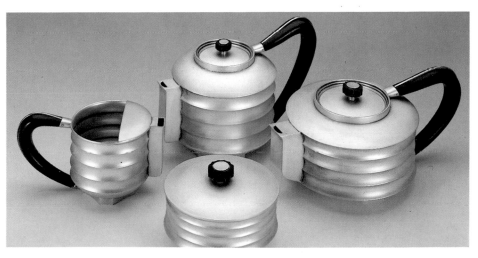

Five flatware services designed by Johan Rohde, Gundorph Albertus, and Harald Nielsen between 1915 and 1940 and made by Georg Jensen Sølvsmedie at different times.

"Christofle" or "Puiforcat"; in some cases, several hallmarks were used, including the standard of silver, a company hallmark, the initials or a symbol of the silversmith, and the piece's number within a series. This last number can be useful because by referring to the catalogue of the company that made the piece,

the date the piece was made can be ascertained with good approximation.

Silver in the 1940s

Because of the Second World War, the 1940s present not so much a decade of silver production as a five-year period. The first years of the decade saw fur-

ther development in the silver production of the United States, most of it a continuation of styles from the preceding decade, but with the addition of decorations based on curving lines. Putting aside various uncertainties, these American works prefigure the design schemes that were repeated in the 1950s:

*Below and bottom:
Silver flatware, part of
a complete service
designed by Georg
Jensen in 1919 and pro-
duced by the Georg
Jensen Sølvsmedie after
1945. The decoration is
based on plant motifs*

*and fully rounded
beading; the hollows of
the knife handles are
filled with decoration of
the same motifs.*

roundish shapes, interpretations of figural forms, a
certain exaggeration that
later came to be called the
Hollywood style, and, finally, patriotic themes, such as
the eagle and stars.

20th-century flatware

During the closing years of
the 19th century and early
years of the 20th, a great
deal of activity took place
in terms of the shapes,
functions and types of flatware. This activity led to
the overcoming of the
design and stylistic sterility
that had marked most of
the 19th-century models.
Several of the factors that
contributed to this state of
affairs had an influence on
much of the silver made in

the years to come. In the
first place was a large,
ongoing cultural debate
that embraced the entire

field of the decorative arts
and that led to a radical
break with the past with
the establishment of new

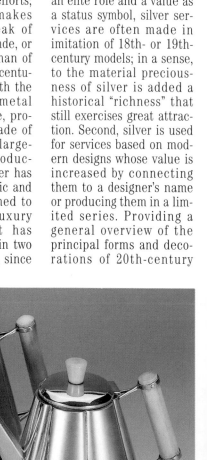

languages and an independence from historical ties. This was translated in the progressive abandonment of forms and models of 18th-century derivation in favour of new forms and decorations with roots growing from the various experiences presented by avant-garde artists and groups; reference to the works of Van de Velde, Mackintosh and Hoffmann were as logical as obvious. These artists and groups are also interesting because they paved the way for the appearance of a new figure, one destined to become the leader in the silver production of the 20th century: the designer. Although most designer flatware is made by hand, the rigorous scientific methods applied to its design provide in embryonic form the information needed for eventual mass production. In most cases, the forms and decorations of 20th-century flatware are the fruit not of shared stylistic tendencies but rather of individual efforts; in this regard it makes more sense to speak of Hoffmann, Ponti, Rohde, or Puiforcat flatware than of Art Nouveau or 20th-century style. Together with the silver and other metal alloys already in use, progressive use was made of stainless steel for large-scale industrial production. The use of silver has become more sporadic and most often is confined to the creation of luxury objects. This fact has affected production in two different ways. First, since silver has again taken on an elite role and a value as a status symbol, silver services are often made in imitation of 18th- or 19th-century models; in a sense, to the material preciousness of silver is added a historical "richness" that still exercises great attraction. Second, silver is used for services based on modern designs whose value is increased by connecting them to a designer's name or producing them in a limited series. Providing a general overview of the principal forms and decorations of 20th-century

flatware is difficult since, as has been pointed out, the style of a given designer is quite often more striking than any shared stylistic element. Even so, and putting aside all the many exceptions, certain tendencies can be noted, in particular a fondness for simple, linear geometric forms that show a greater attention to the functional aspects of flatware than to any stylistic or decorative concerns. The decorations, still found on some models up to the 1930s but destined to disappear completely, repeat stylistic elements of Art Nouveau and Art Deco but tend to be discreet, often confined to the end portions of handles to complete a form.

The use of a variety of materials continued and became even more frequent at the beginning of the century: coral, ivory and semi-precious stones were used to create contrasts on silver surfaces. The adoption of steel blades, strong and sharp, brought a preference for rounded points, and the

desire for a design continuity between the blade and handle is often very much in evidence. The fork was made with three or four prongs, but these became shorter and more pointed. The spoon, as usual, was made in the same design as the fork and usually had a shallower bowl, constructed

185

geometrically in the form of a circle or oval.

The 1950s

Once past the final adversities, the last holdover problems of the world war, the world entered a period of great activity: in Europe there was reconstruction; in North America the United States rose to the rank of superpower. This activity found outlet in the production of objects never before seen: everything had to be new, everything had to be marked by fashion, and the fashions came and went, following one another quickly, as consumerism began its surge forward, due to crack, and then only partially, in the 1970s. The field of silver can be divided into four different lines of production: traditional pieces based on past styles; fashionable pieces made by celebrated design houses; those tied to rising designers; and finally pieces based on a reworking of rationalist designs. The financial well-being of the middle class of this second postwar period led to a demand more for "stylish" objects than modern styles. There was, naturally, continuing production of elegant silver, which is to say pieces based on the neoclassical, Empire, or simplified rococo. The skill of silversmiths creating such traditional examples is sometimes so great that the pieces are almost perfect copies of original models. In some cases, however, the versions are merely simplified interpretations, modest works far removed from the interpretations made earlier during the eclectic period. It was the great design houses for silver, such as Christofle and Jensen, that employed specialized artists who created the pieces that laid the basis of the style of these years. As for Christofle, the firm produced pieces designed by Lino Sabattini in which functionality was wed to a refined elegance: these are essential forms in which the general lines are based on ovals that assume a dynamic aspect, striking but always smooth. Tea services, kettles, decorative vases and so on are in oval forms with grooves, deep fluting and handles that participate in the lines of the body, all in a unitary context in which plastic and fluid lines are favoured and in which any reference to decoration is banished. The works in silver made by the George Jensen factory based on the creative skill of Henning Koppel are based on the absolute value of the line, as in the cup of 1951, the carafe of

Below: Tea and coffee service of the "Como" design by Lino Sabattini and produced by Christofle, Paris, 1950s. Each piece is of an irregular form that is part of a common theme.

Below: Tea and coffee service of the "Como" design by Lino Sabattini and produced by Christofle, Paris, 1950s. Each piece is of an irregular form that is part of a common theme.

Bottom: Teapot designed by Lino Sabattini for Christofle, Paris, 1960. Shaped like a flattened sphere, the body has a funnel spout and long handle attached with hooks.

1952, and the fish bowl of 1954, which is a novel conception since it is completely smooth with the ends of the cover giving the impression of a fish's mouth. Mention should also be made of the vast assortment of inspired silver pieces available from the catalogues of the Berndorf Metalwarengesellshaft Co.

Berndorf made table pieces in steel, nickel silver, and nickel brass, but nothing prevented the occasional variant in silver. In Italy, a series of silver companies, such as Broggi, Calderoni, Sambonet, Valsoldo, Ricci, Cesa, Miracoli, etc., was joined by the work of designers. The eleventh triennial of Milan in 1951, which took place in an atmosphere of economic rebirth throughout the world, provided room for a section called "household metals," in which new silver designs were presented for comparison. The names of Giò Ponti, Roberto Sambonet, Luigi Massoni, Sergio Asti, Enzo Mari, the Castiglioni brothers joined those of Egon Pfeiffer, William Frederick, Carlo Alessi, Wilhelm Wagenfeld, and many others, representing a stylistic and cultural period of great significance in the panorama of high-quality silver production. The 1950s also saw the rediscovery of silver from the modern movements, or at least those defined as rationalist. These include reworkings of Hoffmann, Olbrich, and Christopher Dresser models, as well as examples designed at the Bauhaus by Marianne Brandt, objects of daily use with essential, timeless lines that are as fascinating as the metal of which they are made.

GLOSSARY

Assay The operation of testing silver to establish its level of purity. The assaying is usually followed by the application of a hallmark guaranteeing the quality of the metal.

Assay mark Hallmark used to identify the assayer responsible for assaying an object of silver; also called date letter in England because the marks used were the letters of the alphabet, changing the letter every year.

Beading Decoration obtained using a continuous or interrupted series of small spheres or hemispheres, used in particular for the decoration of borders and edges.

Bean-motif Ornamental decoration consisting of bean motifs or the reproduction of stylized plant pods arranged in various ways, in groups or in spreading rays.

Britannia Standard Hallmark used in Great Britain between 1697 and 1720 to mark pieces of silver and guarantee the standard of 95.8 per cent fine silver. See page 64.

Buffet of plate Display of

impressive and precious objects, including works in silver, in the dining halls of nobility and royal courts during the Middle Ages and later.

Burin Small steel scalpel used for incising metal employed in various decorative techniques, such as engraving, niello and chasing.

Burnishing Method of polishing metals by rubbing the surface with a hard, smooth object.

Cartouche Ornamental motif in imitation of an oval or oblong strip of paper or parchment with fringed or embellished borders within which initials, coats or arms, or dedications are often engraved.

Caryatid Representation of a female figure used in place of a column or other vertical element.

Castor Container used to "cast" sugar, salt, or pepper or to preserve mustard. See pages 52 and 53.

Chasing A technique for working the surface of metal using special tools (burins or gravers) to obtain low-relief ornamental motifs. See page 18.

Chinoiserie European style of decoration using figurative motifs inspired by Chinese art, particularly popular in silver during the late 17th and mid 18th centuries. See page 35.

Claw and ball Type of foot support shaped like a claw gripping a sphere.

Damascene The art of decorating iron, steel, or bronze with inlaid threads of gold or silver that are hammered into lines engraved in the metal using a burin to create a decorative design.

Date letter See Assay mark

Embossing Technique of working plate by hammering from the reverse so that a decoration projects in relief; finished on the front by chasing. Also called repoussé. See page 10.

Engraving Technique for creating decorative motifs by cutting fine grooves with a sharp tool. Often used to apply heraldic decoration and initials to smooth surfaces. See page 18.

Epergne Large table centerpiece composed of a central basket and several smaller baskets arranged on the sides and usually removable. Epergnes were used from the middle of the 18th century onward for the display and service at table of fruit and sweets. See page 90.

Festoon Decorative motif usually shaped like a chain or strip hanging between two points; festoons can be composed of branches, flowers, and leaves and are sometimes associated with other elements, such as masks or ribbons.

Filigree Procedure in goldworking consisting of weaving thin threads of metal and soldering them at points of contact. See page 42.

Finial Highest element of an object, often of great sculptural value, often associated with the function of acting as a grip for raising the cover.

Flatware Generic term for tableware: spoons, forks, knives and other cutlery; compare hollow ware.

Fluting Shallow rounded parallel grooves used on the shafts of classical columns and applied to silver, as on candlestick stems.

Gadrooning Decoration, usually applied to borders, composed of convex curves or inverted fluting.

Gilding Procedure for covering a piece or silver or part of it with a thin layer of gold as a form of decoration and protection.

Grotesque A combination of various decorative elements used in the Roman period, usually fanciful or fantastic human and animal forms interwoven with foliage, rediscovered and widely used during the Renaissance period.

Hallmark The official mark impressed on a piece of silver by an assay office or guild as a guarantee; also the mark of the maker of the object.

Hollow ware Generic term for all vessel forms, especially those with significant depth and volume.

Lambrequin Decorative motif of deeply scalloped stylized fringelike motifs, often associated with shells or palmettes, used in particular in France during the early 18th century.

Mask Decorative element shaped like a mask, usually grotesque, often used to hide a fitting, as of a handle.

Molding Element projecting from the flat surface or from the border of an object used to add a decorative plane or curved strip to the object.

Moresque Decoration based on Near Eastern art and similar to the arabesque, composed of scrolling stylized foliage.

Niello Ornamentation obtained by filling incised lines in the surface of silver with a mixture composed of silver, red copper, lead and sulfur; the resulting surface is inlaid with an enamellike design. See page 9.

Parcel-gilt Silver that has been gilded only in certain areas.

Plate Precious metal, especially silver bullion, and thus a generic term for wrought silver; derived from the Spanish *plata*, meaning "silver."

Repoussé See Embossing

Sterling Standard for silver alloy used in England composed of 92.5 per cent pure silver and 7.5 per cent of another metal.

Vermeil See Gilt

INDEX OF NAMES

Numbers in *italics* refer to illustrations.

Credits

The text of the chapter on 19th-century silver and the black-and-white drawings were prepared by Maurizio De Paoli. The author and publishers extend special thanks to Christie's, Finarte and Sotheby's auction houses and the antiquarians Carlo Teardo and Gianfranco Mazzoleni of Milan.

The translator thanks Gérard Desgranges for assistance with the French texts.

The abbreviations a (above), b (bottom), c (center), l (left), and r (right) refer to the position of the illustration on the page.

Amsterdam, Historisch Museum: 15a, 151
Athens, National Archaeological Museum: 8
Cesena, Museo Storico dell'Antichità, Biblioteca Malatestiana (photo by Ivano Giovannini): 12b
Christie's: Geneva 16l, 18, 28, 33, 38c, 50, 51, 55, 57b, 62, 68l, 70, 77b, 80l, 83a, 88, 102b, 104, 105a, 110b, 113, 120b, 123l, 130a, 145b, 152l, 153b, 167, 168b, 171, 174, 176b, 178; New York 165, 173ar, 173b, 175, 182, 183; Rome 151a
Copenhagen, Nationalmuseet: 12a
Finarte, Milan: 30, 31, 35, 37, 43b, 45b, 54, 57a, 59, 60l, 61l, 67l, 68r, 71r, 75, 78a, 80r, 81, 84b, 85, 86, 89, 93, 96, 97, 98, 99, 101b, 102a, 103a, 105b, 106, 107, 108b, 110a, 112, 124, 128, 129a, 130b, 131, 132a, 133b, 134, 136, 140b, 142b, 143r, 143l, 144l, 147b, 152r, 168a, 169, 172, 173al, 179a, 181, 184, 185
Herzoglich Sachsen Coburg und Gothasche Hauptverwaltung, Coburg: 14
Madrid, Museo Arqueòlogico Nacional: 9
Mazzoleni, Gianfranco, Milan: 26, 73r
Mazzoleni (photos by Cesare Somaini, Milan): 76, 84a, 108a, 126b, 151b, 156l, 157, 158al, 158b, 166, 170
Museo Archeologico, Naples (photo by Luciano Pedicini, Naples): 11
Museo di Capodimonte, Naples (photo by Luciano Pedicini, Naples): 17
Rome, Museo di Palazzo Venezia: 19a
Saint-Denis, Musée Bouilhet Christofle: 20a (photo Kollar), 20b, 187
Sotheby's: Geneva 19br, 19bl, 63r, 120a; London 15r, 16l, 23a, 24, 25, 32a, 34, 44, 45a, 48, 52, 53, 60r, 79, 118a, 135l, 140a, 146r, 147a, 154l; Munich 176a, 177, 179b, 180, 186; New York 22, 23b, 27, 29a, 29b, 32b, 38a, 42, 43a, 47, 49, 61r, 66, 69, 71l, 74, 82, 83b, 87, 90, 103b, 109, 111, 119l, 123r, 127, 129b, 132b, 133a, 135r, 141, 146l, 150ar, 150al, 153a, 154r, 155, 159, 162, 163, 164
Teardo, Carlo, Milan: 46, 56, 63l, 67r, 72, 73l, 77a, 78b, 91, 100, 101a, 118b, 119r, 122, 125, 126a, 142a, 143a, 144r, 145a, 150b, 156r, 158ar